Everyday Conversation

About this series...

Series Editors: Mark L. Knapp & John A. Daly,
both at the University of Texas

Designed for college and university undergraduates, the **Interpersonal Commtexts** series will also interest a much larger general audience. Ideal as basic or supplementary texts, these volumes are suited for courses in the development and practice of interpersonal skills; verbal and nonverbal behavior (the basis of interpersonal transactions); functions of communication in face-to-face interaction; the development of interpersonal behavior at various points in the lifespan; and intergroup and intercultural aspects of interpersonal communication. Readable and comprehensive, the **Interpersonal Commtexts** describe contexts within which interpersonal communication takes place and provide ways to study and understand the interpersonal communication process.

In this series...

Everyday Conversation

Robert E. Nofsinger

INTERPERSONAL COMMTEXTS 1

SAGE PUBLICATIONS
The International Professional Publishers
Newbury Park   London   New Delhi

For information address:

 SAGE Publications, Inc.
2455 Teller Road
Newbury Park, California 91320

BJ
2121
· N64
1991

SAGE Publications Ltd.
6 Bonhill Street
London EC2A 4PU
United Kingdom

SAGE Publications India Pvt. Ltd.
M-32 Market
Greater Kailash I
New Delhi 110 048 India

Printed in the United States of America

Library of Congress Cataloging-in-Publication Data

Nofsinger, Robert E.
    Everyday conversation / by Robert E. Nofsinger
        p.   cm — (Interpersonal commtexts 1)
    Includes bibliographical references and index
    ISBN 0-8039-3309-6. — ISBN 0-8039-3310-X (pbk.)
    1. Conversation. I. Title. II. Series.
BJ2121.N64 1990
302.3'46—dc20   90-20314
                                                            CIP

FIRST PRINTING, 1991

Sage Production Editor: Astrid Virding

Contents

To Mary

Preface

Among the books currently available on conversational processes, *Everyday Conversation* fills a specific niche. It is a textbook written by a single author (rather than a collection of research studies). It addresses important processes and characteristics of conversation in the analytical language used by scholars, explaining that language along the way. Yet it is aimed at advanced college undergraduates (juniors and seniors), as well as beginning graduate students. Important concepts are emphasized with italics at their introduction and are thoroughly illustrated with examples. The strengths of the book can be described as follows.

The primary discussions are illustrated by segments of real-life talk. In every case, I have satisfied myself that data segments are from actual people interacting in the normal course of their everyday lives. Most of these segments come from tape recordings or from published studies that have used recordings as their data. In a few cases, I have used segments from field notes that were produced at about the same time as the talk.

Note, however, that in the discussion—but not in the data segments—I have occasionally invented contrasting examples to clarify certain points. The advantage of using transcripts of naturally occurring talk is that conversation is designed to accomplish practical goals and to work interactively in ways that invented or artificially manipulated talk is not. Writers' and researchers' imaginations cannot do justice to the delicacy and complexity of ordinary conversation. Data segments should be read in conjunction with the Appendix, which describes the transcription notation.

Conversation is described here predominantly from one perspective, that of conversation analysis. The focus is on sequencing and structure, a systemic or sociological approach, rather than on psychological factors and internal variables. I believe that such an approach will equip students of conversation to extend their understanding from a variety of perspectives and methods. The main exception to this unitary approach is that Chapter 2 is based on ordinary language philosophy in general and speech act theory in particular. My purpose in that chapter is to emphasize that conversation is not merely the communication of information, but the performance of social actions directed by the participants at one another. Speech act theory stresses this point very clearly and, at the same time, I am able to introduce the reader to a major contrasting approach. In an attempt to narrow the gap between these perspectives, I have recast speech act theory from its focus on the speaker's intentions to a greater emphasis on the listener's inferences about those intentions. Still, an adjustment needs to be made by the reader when moving on to Chapter 3, which switches from the rational (intuitive, mentalistic) mind-set of speech act theory to the empirical (observational) approach of conversation analysis.

In addition to noting the absence of other recognized perspectives (primarily laboratory-experimental and discourse-analytic perspectives), certain other warnings are in order. Because of limitations on the length of the manuscript, several important aspects of conversation have either been omitted or given only brief treatment. Most obvious in their absence are the integration of verbal and nonverbal behaviors, conversational coherence (which has been extensively treated in Craig & Tracy, 1983a), and topic organization. And, although this book takes a conversation-analytic perspective, it is neither an actual conversation analysis nor a methodological prescription for one. Finally, the specific details of conversational patterning are important to a working understanding of this basic form of interpersonal communication. Those details are embodied in the data segments and the accompanying point-by-point discussions. To benefit fully from this book, the reader will have to study the data segments and refer back to them when reading the discussion! To encourage this conspiracy between my writing and the reader's thinking, I have used the inclusive pronoun *we* in all chapters.

I gratefully acknowledge the continuing encouragement, support, and assistance of Mary Nofsinger, whose love and devotion carry the day. I also acknowledge, with thanks, the contributions of book series editors Mark Knapp and John Daly at the University of Texas, Wes Shellen (my colleague at Montana), Bill Ausmus and Kitty Carlsen (my graduate students), and other colleagues and students who have made suggestions for improvement of the manuscript. Thanks also go to Alex Tan, director of the School of Communication at Washington State University, for his support.

This book is dedicated, with love, to Mary M. Nofsinger.

Robert E. Nofsinger

Introduction

Everyone can conduct ordinary conversation—or so it seems. The immense power of everyday talk is at our disposal to contact and influence other people: to enlist their help, to offer them companionship, to protect ourselves from their demands, to establish important relationships with them, and to present ourselves as having the qualities that they (and we) admire. Almost everything we do that concerns other people involves us in conversation. And yet we all experience problems during conversation that threaten to embarrass us or prevent us from reaching our immediate and long-term goals. We find ourselves unable to "get a word in edgewise," or to get others to talk about things of special interest to us. We are forced to say something when we would prefer to remain silent, or to listen when we would rather daydream. We think that we made ourselves clear, but have an uneasy feeling that others did not understand us. And the worst part of it is that we are uncertain why we are

having these difficulties—or how we manage to be so successful most of the time. This by itself is an important reason to
study the basic processes of ordinary talk. As participants, we
may be able to improve our performance by learning some of
the technical details of how conversation works, by taking
advantage of its dynamics. But there are other important reasons for students of interpersonal communication to investigate conversation.

One reason is that conversation works so well. Participants
are overwhelmingly successful in ordering and interpreting
their talk for themselves and for each other, especially when we
take into account that most conversational troubles are resolved
smoothly and quickly. Given that people do not have direct
access to each other's thoughts, and given that conversation
works even among people with widely differing purposes,
backgrounds, and social positions, everyday talk represents a
tremendous feat of coordination! If we are to understand interpersonal communication, we need to learn how this is accomplished so successfully.

Another reason is that the techniques and patterns that people use in conversation form the basis for other more "official"
and more noticeable types of interaction (such as interviewing
for a job, testifying in court, holding a group meeting, or par-
ticipating in a broadcast news interview or talk show). People
do not adopt a totally new or different system for communicating in these more formal, controlled, or task-oriented episodes.
Instead, they *adapt* their system of conversational interaction to
fit these other circumstances. We learn conversation first and
then apply our conversational skills to other forms of interactive talk.

Still another reason is that conversation is a major part of
everyday life and functions to organize society itself. Sociolo-
gists such as Douglas (1970), Goffman (1971, 1981), and Karp
and Yoels (1986) have recognized that the orderliness of everyday life forms the basis of society's structure. That orderliness
is generated in social interaction, primarily conversation.

Finally, conversation is a primary method through which interpersonal relationships are formed, maintained, and dissolved. We become acquaintances through conversation. Through conversation, we establish and strengthen friendships and peer relationships. Our family life is created and enacted each day through conversation. And, in large part, we find employment (or fail to) and achieve success on the job (or fail to) through our everyday talk. Conversation matters!

So the conduct of ordinary, everyday conversation holds a vitally important place in human society. It is through conversation that we build and maintain contacts with people and carry out the business of everyday life. Although this ordinary talk often seems effortless to us, the resulting conversation is usually complex and intricately designed. In fact, there is so much to study, and so many approaches to it have been developed, that in this book we will rely primarily on a single perspective: the approach known as conversation analysis. We will also draw briefly upon the study of language pragmatics in this chapter and more specifically on speech act theory in Chapter 2. But other types of research on conversation are beyond the scope of this book. Let us begin our study of this basic communication process by examining what conversation is and what (if anything) is "ordinary" about it.

❏ Everyday Conversation

One primary characteristic of conversation is that it is fully *interactive*. At least two people must participate in it, and they exchange messages on a real-time basis. Participants take turns in exchanging these messages, so conversation is fundamentally a sequential activity. Talk is designed to reflect back on prior turns and project ahead to future ones, and we interpret talk as if it is tied in some way to prior and future turns. Furthermore, all participants are eligible to take turns as speaker and to make substantive contributions to the conversation—whether they actually do so or not. Thus a professor meeting with a group of students to confirm that the preparations for a class project have been made is engaging in a conversation with them, but during a class lecture, those same people are not having a *conversation* because the students have more restricted rights to speak in that situation. The talk is not as fully and immediately interactive. And participants in conversation routinely monitor each other and often respond to each other in delicately coordinated ways.

Conversation is commonplace and practical.

A second primary characteristic of conversation is that it is *locally managed.* The participants themselves, during the course of their interaction, determine which people get to speak, in what order they speak, and for how long. The things people are expected to talk about, what they actually say, and how they say it are also worked out among the participants as the conversation progresses. This contrasts with such other forms of talk as formal debate, in which the order and length of speaking turns are decided upon before the event even begins, and drama, in which the actual words people speak may be scripted (written down). The organization and content of a conversation are not predetermined or planned in any specific way (although, as we shall see later, participants do orient toward certain rules of conversational conduct).

A third important characteristic of conversation is that it is *mundane.* That is, conversation is commonplace and practical. One sense in which this is true is that conversation pervades our daily lives. We are repeatedly engaged in talking informally with others throughout the day, sometimes briefly, sometimes at length, about matters of varying degrees of importance. And even when we engage in talk that departs from these characteristics of conversation, we use many of the same practices and patterns (often in modified form) that we use in conversation. As indicated above, research is showing that conversation serves as the foundation, the mundane basis, for other forms of communication and for social organization generally (Atkinson, 1982; Heritage, 1984b). Another way in which conversation is mundane is that we use the most pervasive and common of communication systems—language—to conduct it. Of course there are many nonverbal components in most conversations (gestures, eye contact, variations in the voice, and so on) and these are pervasive in our everyday interaction, just as language is. But note how many of these it is possible to get along without when we speak on the phone, or for some other reason converse without actually seeing the other participants. In this book, we will focus on spoken language as the vehicle for conducting conversation.[1]

❑ Pragmatics

The study of linguistic communication, of actual language use in specific situations, is known as *pragmatics*. Since conversation is the predominant form of oral language use, we will rely on certain concepts and theories from pragmatics and related discourse studies. This perspective differs from other approaches to the study of language in that it focuses on how speakers design their talk to convey particular social actions, how that talk is interpreted by listeners as having the status of certain actions that the speakers are producing, how participants make inferences about what meanings are being conveyed on that particular occasion, how participants' sense of appropriateness can be used to produce special communicative effects, how participants organize their talk, and so forth. That is, pragmatics focuses on the practical operation of linguistic messages being used by people in actual communicative situations. Levinson (1983, chap. 1) provides a technical discussion of several definitions. The approach of pragmatics thus contrasts with the study of a language's system of sounds (phonology), its rules for constructing correct or valid words and

sentences (morphology and syntax), and its system for repre-
senting meaning in linguistic form (semantics). Pragmatics is
the study of how we *use* these various as-
pects of language to accomplish our goals
and do communicative work.

*Everyday
conversation is
a collection of
language games.*

LANGUAGE GAMES

One way of looking at language as it is
used in everyday conversation is to think
of it as a collection of language *games*.[2]
The idea is to apply what we know about ordinary, everyday
games (chess, checkers, tic-tac-toe, card games, competitive
sports, and so on) to the conduct of conversation. For example,
we know that every game has a defined set of behaviors, often
called *moves*, through which people play the game. In most
board games the players actually move pieces from one place
to another in order to make a move. Many card games, on the
other hand, have two different kinds of moves: a verbal one in
which players bet or bid and a nonverbal one in which cards
are played or discarded. In general, players take *turns* making
these moves and attempt to achieve some *goal*, which is the
point of the game itself. The goal of most sports games is to
outscore one's opponent. Moves are functionally designed to
contribute to the attainment of the goal in various ways. The
issue of which move or moves to make at some particular time
in the game is referred to as the question of *tactics*, or sometimes
strategy. Using a full-court press to get the ball back in basket-
ball, using sideline passes to conserve time on the clock in
football, and occupying the corner cells in tic-tac-toe are examples of tactics. In this book, we will call the localized question
of "what to do now" *tactics*, and reserve the term *strategy* for the
overall "game plan," if any. The elements of the game, its
boundaries, and constraints on players are specified by various
kinds of *rules* that, in effect, create the framework or logic
within which the game is played. One result of viewing conversation in this way is that we tend to see it as a rational activity

having a strategic dimension. Another is that we can more readily make sense of conversational events by applying our extensive knowledge of games.

STRATEGIC ACTION

The moves of conversation are produced primarily through talk. Participants are not merely *saying* something to each other when they talk. They are *doing* something at the same time: directing communicative or social actions at one another. People greet, congratulate, invite, criticize, and insult each other; these are some of the moves of conversation. In fact, participants talk primarily for the purpose of producing such actions. The relationship between what someone actually says and the action he or she is performing is a complicated one, as we shall see. Conversational actions are actually *interpretations* of participants' utterances. For example, consider the following segment of conversation, in which a district attorney and a public defender are engaged in plea bargaining:

(1.1) [Maynard, 1984, p. 191][3]
 1 DA: Uh I'll give you ninety days with credit for time served
 2 PD: Nah that's no good

In utterance 1, the district attorney is not merely saying that he will give the public defender's client ninety days—he is making an *offer* to do so. And in utterance 2, the public defender is performing a *rejection* of that offer.

Jacobs (1985; Jacobs & Jackson, 1983a) argues that we are able to recognize what actions our fellow participants are producing because we understand the language game in which we are involved. That is, we know, either explicitly or tacitly, what general goals people are pursuing when they engage in a certain sort of conversation. In the above instance, participants know that the general point of plea bargaining is to come to an agreement on how to dispose of the case. In fact, plea bargaining is defined in terms of that overall goal, what Craig (1986,

p. 266) calls a "formal" goal. We also know what sorts of moves (social or communicative actions) are useful or even essential to reaching that goal and some of the ways in which those moves might be produced through language. In the plea bargaining example, the lawyers know that one of them must eventually propose a specific way of disposing of the case, they know that one way of doing this is to make an offer, and they know what to say to produce such an action. Furthermore, each knows that if strategic or tactical considerations dictate, the other might be prompted to make the offer if it is solicited, as in Segment 1.2.

(1.2) [Maynard, 1984, p. 85]
1 PD: Is there an offer in that case
2 DA: Yeah a reckless with a deuce ((drunk driving)) dispo

Here, PD solicits an offer from DA and, in line 2, DA offers a "deuce dispo" (a drunk driving disposition of the case). As our conversational partners talk to us, we are able to interpret what action a given utterance ought to be by applying our understanding of what has been done so far, what needs to be done, what the utterance seems designed to do, what alternative actions might have been performed at this point in the conversation, and so on. Notice that in different circumstances, constituting a different language game, our interpretation of what action is being produced by a given utterance ought to be different. For example, if utterance 1 (the "ninety days" line) in Data Segment 1.1 were spoken by a judge to a recently convicted defendant (instead of by one lawyer to another), it might very well be interpreted as the action of imposing sentence. In this case, "Nah that's no good" might be regarded as arrogant or disrespectful, since the rules of that language game do not permit the convicted person to reject the sentence.

Even when a conversation cannot usefully be regarded as a specific type of language game with an official purpose (Craig's formal goal), it is clear that participants often attribute some purpose to each other's talk. A person's utterances are regarded as steps in his or her strategic plan for attaining an individual goal, which Craig (1986, pp. 266-268; Craig & Tracy, 1983b, p. 15) calls a "strategic" goal. Here, too, the interpretation of what action is being produced seems to be a problem-solving process in which participants' common-sense reasoning is used to identify communicative actions in the stream of talk and relate them to the speaker's presumed goals (Jacobs, 1985, p. 336). For example, if a woman assumes that a certain guy intends to arrange a date with her, she is likely to interpret his questions

> *During a sequence of turns participants exchange social or communicative actions.*

and statements about various forthcoming events as "probes" designed to find out what she likes. But regardless of whether participants' actions and intentions are inferred from an overall sense of the rules, moves, and ultimate (formal) goal of the particular language game, or from a sense of the participants' personal strategic goals and the plans that might bring those goals about, it is clear that conversational interaction exhibits recurrent patterns that can be studied in detail. The ability to recognize and anticipate these patterns can be a powerful means to influence the course and outcome of conversation.

CONVERSATIONAL PATTERNS

Careful study of conversation and other forms of interactive talk over the last two decades has revealed "organized patterns of stable, identifiable structural features . . . [that] stand independently of the psychological or other characteristics of particular speakers" (Heritage, 1984b, p. 241). As participants take turns responding to one another's conversational actions, their talk develops in systematic ways that can be recognized, described, and used for communicative purposes. Speakers design their utterances for certain aspects of the context, especially for who the other participants are and what they have just said. This process is called *recipient design* (Sacks & Schegloff,

1979). At the same time that speakers shape their utterances specifically for the intended recipient(s), their utterances also contribute to the unfolding of that context in a way that sustains or alters it (Heritage, 1984b, p. 242). Because of the reciprocal relationships among the various turns, utterances, and actions of conversation, talk becomes organized in recognizable ways. For example, many communicative actions occur in pairs (such as greeting-greeting, question-answer, or invitation-acceptance). Larger conversational structures (such as negotiations, arguments, or stories) may be composed of various arrangements of such pairs. Utterances in conversation are also recognizably connected to each other in topical ways. That is, groups of utterances seem to "be about the same topic," a characteristic called *coherence* (Craig & Tracy, 1983b, p. 14). And there often seem to be typical utterance "shapes" for producing certain actions. Much of our exploration in this book will focus on such conversational patterns.

CONCLUDING REMARKS

Conversation is a process in which people interact on a moment-by-moment, turn-by-turn basis. During a sequence of turns participants exchange talk with each other, but, more important, they exchange social or communicative actions. These actions are the "moves" of conversation considered as a collection of games. Indeed, conversational actions are some of the most important moves of the broader "game of everyday life." The rest of this book is an exploration of the techniques and patterns through which participants display to each other what it is they are doing (which version of the language game they are engaged in, what acts they are producing, and so on). The chapters are arranged so that each builds upon earlier ones.

❑ Organization of the Book

In the chapters that follow, we will begin to study the details of how people conduct conversation. Chapter 2 discusses conversational action, what makes an utterance an act, how such acts may be implied (we will say "implicated") rather than performed directly, and other selected matters related to pragmatics and speech act theory. In Chapter 3, we examine how conversational actions are organized into sequences, how the acts of a particular sequence are related to each other, and how sequences themselves may be organized with respect to other sequences. This and subsequent chapters draw heavily upon conversation-analytic research. Chapter 4 focuses on the system of taking turns in conversation and contrasts it to the turn-taking practices used in other selected forms of talk. We will discover that many conversational patterns are closely related to the processes of the turn-taking system. In Chapter 5, participants' methods for repairing mistakes and misunderstandings are described. We will also examine some ways in which participants attempt to guide each other to (or away from) particular interpretations of their talk. Here, the issue is how we align our actions and understandings during the course of ongoing conversation. Finally, in Chapter 6, we take a brief look at arguments and stories as examples of larger patterns commonly found in ordinary conversation and at how they are constructed utilizing the practices we have previously discussed. Throughout the book, we will be primarily interested in *how* people conduct the conversations they do, and what they can be seen to accomplish socially or communicatively. We will generally avoid speculating as to *why* (in a psychological sense) they conduct their conversations that way. We begin by focusing on individual conversational acts.

❏ **Notes**

1. Although sign (manual) language is a form of natural human language, its use for conversational interaction is beyond the scope of this book.

2. This perspective was used by Wittgenstein (1958) in his studies in pragmatics and has been recommended and used by Jacobs (1985), Jacobs and Jackson (1983a), and Rosenfield, Hayes, and Frentz (1976), among others.

3. The source of each data segment is given in brackets. Special notation used in the segments is explained in the Appendix.

2

Conversational Action

Conversation, as we saw in the introductory chapter, is a process in which the participants direct communicative or social actions toward one another. It is vital that we develop our intuitive and analytic senses of these actions so that we can focus on what people *do* in conversation (their "moves") rather than merely on what they *say*. In this chapter, we take a much closer look at those actions from the perspective of speech act theory and related work in pragmatics. We will find answers (but not the only possible ones) to such questions as, How does a person's talk become his or her conversational action? How can we tell that a person who says one thing actually means another? How are different actions really different from (or similar to) each other? In answering these questions, we will examine in detail the everyday actions that participants call promises and requests, and look more briefly at offers, invitations, statements, and other ordinary actions.

❏ Speech Acts

Chapter 1 proposed the idea of thinking of conversation as a game or collection of games. Putting that idea to work, we understand that a successful field-goal kicker in the game of American football has accomplished three things: kicked the ball (when we look at it one way), made a field goal (looking at it another way), and made the coach happy (looking at it a third way). Similarly, when conversational participants talk, we can see them as doing several distinguishable things at once. Our first step will be to sort these out, before concentrating on one in particular. Consider the following exchange between two college women, one of whom is about to eat a sandwich.

(2.1) [Craig & Tracy, 1983a, B-K, p. 304][1]
  5 B: Are you sure that you don't want half? This is huge.
  6 K: No. Thanks. (I've finally) got my apple.

In line 5, B accomplishes several things through her speaking. One is that she produces a message with a certain linguistic (semantic and syntactic) meaning, an interrogative sentence that "asks" whether K desires part of the sandwich. (Note, however, that the question mark designates upward voice inflection rather than a certain type of sentence—see the Appendix.) Looking at it another way, a second thing that B does is to make an *offer*, an offer to share her sandwich with K. And third, B may have produced some effect on K. For example, she may have made K feel appreciated; and we can imagine that she might have persuaded K to take a portion of sandwich, although as it turned out she did not. Let us examine and give names to these things that B does, beginning with her speaking that meaningful message.

UTTERANCES

It would be tempting to call "Are you sure that you don't want half" a sentence. The problem with this is that *sentence* is a technical term in linguistics that normally refers to an abstract grammatical structure, rather than to an actual concrete message. In addition, while this particular message is certainly sentencelike, people often speak in ways that depart from the sentence ideal and yet remain perfectly understandable. Consequently, we shall call the linguistically meaningful message that a person speaks during conversation an *utterance*.[2] So B (in the example above) is producing an utterance that conveys a certain meaning. For example, "you" refers to K, "sure" has a certain semantic meaning having to do with being certain about something, "want" and "half" each have particular meanings in this message, and so on. Austin (1975) describes this sort of behavior as an act of "saying something," and he terms it "the performance of a locutionary act" (p. 94).[3] His concept of *locutionary act* (our term is *utterance*) is designed to distinguish the actual speaking of a linguistically meaningful message from the performance of a different sort of act. This second notion of "act" is his primary interest—and will be our primary interest in this chapter and throughout much of the book. We can initially characterize this distinction as the difference between saying something and (in saying it) doing something.

ILLOCUTIONARY ACTS

When B, in the "sandwich" conversation (Segment 2.1), *said* "Are you sure that you don't want half," she was also *doing* an offer to K. Austin (1975, pp. 98-101) calls this doing of a social or communicative action an *illocutionary act*. Recalling the idea of language games from Chapter 1, we can see that illocutionary acts are the moves of the game. Just as the football player kicks the ball in order to produce a field goal, so a person speaks an utterance (Austin's locutionary act) in order to produce a communicative action (Austin's illocutionary act). In a casual conversation among friends, participants will make moves to express recognition of each other, moves to self-disclose about themselves, moves to request information from their conversational partners, moves to offer something desirable (as B did to K), and so forth. We recognize such moves as being in the service of displaying and strengthening the friendships among the participants, a goal that can be thought of either as the formal goal of that particular language game or as a strategic goal of some participant who is implementing plans for achieving it (see Craig, 1986). Note that it is not merely the saying of an intelligible utterance, but the production and interpretation of that utterance *as an illocutionary act* that makes it a move in the game. In the following example, B is responsible for a performance that (it seems) A particularly liked.

(2.2) [Pomerantz, 1978, p. 95]
 1   A: Oh it was just <u>beau</u>tiful.
 2   B: Well <u>thank</u> you uh I thought it was quite nice,

In line 1, A produces an utterance that says the performance was beautiful (a locutionary act). But in saying this, A also does something—a *compliment*—directed at B. Note the vocal emphasis indicated on "beau" (and on "thank"). This compliment is the illocutionary act, a move to which B responds with an appreciation ("Well <u>thank</u> you") and an agreement ("I thought it was quite nice") packaged together (Pomerantz, 1978, pp. 83-86). The distinction between what is said and what is thereby done is an important one. In part, this distinction is important because people can produce any given illocutionary act by using several (perhaps many) different sayings. But it is also important to understand this distinction because what participants are really doing in a conversation can sometimes be hidden behind what they say.

Just as it would have been possible for speaker A to do a compliment using a different utterance ("I just <u>loved</u> it," or "You should be very proud of yourself"), so it is possible to produce the other actions of everyday conversation through a variety of spoken forms. This fact raises important issues about the design and interpretation of messages. An illocutionary act is essentially an actional *interpretation* of an utterance. Participants are able to infer that utterances produced in certain ways

are intended to count as particular illocutionary actions. We
will take up some of the factors that seem to guide these interpretations later in the chapter. For now, we will just note that
speech act theory, as begun by Austin in his 1955 lectures at
Harvard, and further developed and systematized by Searle
(1969) and others, has focused on illocutionary acts to such an
extent that the term *speech act* has predominantly come to mean
illocutionary act. We will return to a consideration of the speech
act in this sense after we have described the third thing that
people do when they talk.

EFFECTS

The speech (illocutionary) acts performed by a speaker presumably have some further effects on his or her conversational
partners, just as making a field goal in football has effects on
the players, the coaches, and others. In the "compliment" example above (Data Segment 2.2), A's compliment seems to have
had the effect of pleasing B. So it might be said that, in addition
to doing the action of a compliment, A also performed the "act"
of pleasing B. Austin (1975, p. 101) calls this a *perlocutionary act*.
To avoid confusion among the several senses of act that we have
discussed, we will refer to this as the *effect*, or perlocutionary
effect, of a speech act. Note that perlocutionary effects are not
so much central components of conversation itself as they are
the results of conversation. To be sure, we regard some of these
effects as the goals we are trying to reach through our talk.
Others we regard as unintended and perhaps unwanted results
of our talk. But perlocutionary effects are not themselves talk
in the way that utterances and (illocutionary) speech acts are.
Let us look back at our B-K "sandwich" example (Segment 2.1)
to ferret out the differences. To make an offer, as B offered part
of her sandwich to K, is a speech act. One might, in a stilted sort
of way, say "I hereby offer you . . ." and be doing an offer merely
by saying so. Other participants might be pleased, surprised, or
even angered by that offer, but these are effects of the speech
act of offering, not illocutionary acts themselves. One cannot

achieve these effects merely by saying "I hereby please you," "I hereby surprise you," and so forth. Much of the research in communication, both in classical and contemporary times, has focused on how people may be persuaded, convinced, informed, entertained, and so on. These are all perlocutionary effects, and important ones, at that. Nevertheless, we shall keep our attention on various questions about *how* conversation is conducted, not on what is accomplished through it.

So conversational participants perform utterances in order to produce speech acts, which then may have various intended or unintended effects. Our continuing focus will be on speech acts, since they are the moves through which the games of ordinary conversation (and of everyday life) are played. We next look at how an utterance might come to be defined as a specific speech act.

❏ Conventional Foundations

How do recipients of an utterance know what speech act the speaker is doing? The general answer is that there is a publicly available system that forms a basis for people's design and interpretation of talk. Everyday language users possess certain pragmatic knowledge about how language and conversation work, what the rules are, standard ways of performing speech acts, what people's conversational goals might be expected to be, and the like (see McLaughlin, 1984, pp. 13-34). These expectations are *conventional* in the sense that they are shared among people from the same linguistic and subcultural group. Just as the rules, strategy, and tactics of an ordinary game provide a foundation upon which anyone who wants to play must base his or her behavior, so these pragmatic language conventions provide a foundation for how to use talk in conversation. Searle (1969) has argued that certain characteristics must be present in a speaker's utterance, beliefs, and intentions (and also in the communicative situation) for that utterance to work properly as a promise, request, statement, warning, or other speech act. One way of looking at these conventions is to regard them as a special type of rule that defines or creates—we shall say *constitutes*—the speech act.

CONSTITUTIVE RULES

In any complex conventional social activity, certain elements are created by social agreement. For example, kicking a round ball into a net is not *by itself* a goal (score) in soccer; the rules of soccer make it so by defining what a goal is. Similarly, the little statues on a chess board have certain powers of movement and capture only because the rules of chess create various chess pieces, moves, and so on. Philosophers call this type of rule a *constitutive rule*, and Searle (1969) proposes that the various speech acts we use in everyday life are defined (constituted) by such rules in the pragmatics of language (pp. 33-42). Constitutive rules are distinguished in this scheme from *regulative rules*, the kind that normally come to mind when we think of rules that constrain when and where we may do a particular act. Greetings, for example, should be done when people first make contact (that is, not in the middle of the conversation), initial greetings should be returned (answered), and so on. These conversational requirements are regulative rules (or, more broadly, social norms). By contrast, constitutive rules tell us *how* one can do a greeting—what kind of utterance, spoken under what conditions, would count as a greeting. We will return to a comparison of constitutive and regulative rules later. But now let us examine in detail the conventions that constitute particular speech acts. For example, what characteristics must be present for the recipient of an utterance, the hearer, to interpret it as a promise? [4]

The promise. Searle (1969) presents an extensive analysis of the conditions that constitute the speech (illocutionary) act of promising. Some of these conditions apply to virtually any speech act: that the speaker and hearer are using the same language and dialect, that they are speaking and hearing clearly, and so on. But there are several constitutive rules that are specific to the promise (and related speech acts). These can be categorized as relating to propositional content conditions, situational conditions, sincerity conditions, and what Searle calls the "essential condition" (pp. 57-64).[5]

Some utterances involve making a proposition. In linguistics, a proposition is a meaning that can be "expressed by a declarative sentence" (Stubbs, 1983, p. 203). That is, some utterances make assertions about something; they include one or more propositions. For an utterance to be interpreted as a promise (according to conventional constitutive rules), it must be designed to be *about a future behavior of the speaker*. Notice that we are dealing with the linguistic meaning of the utterance here. So the propositional content (meaning) of an utterance designed as a promise must be that the speaker is going to perform a specific future behavior. Consider the following segment of conversation in which a student is setting up an appointment with her professor to get a registration form signed.

(2.3) [Off-con, DC][6]
  1 S: Okay (1.0) then I'll see you Tuesday.
  2 P: All right. (.) Good.
  3 S: With my little thing all filled out?

If S's utterance in line 1 is to meet the definition of a promise, its meaning must include the proposition that S will do some future behavior. In this case, the utterance states that explicitly: S will see "you" Tuesday. Thus line 1 meets the first condition of the speech act of promising—the *propositional content rule*. It is possible for utterances to meet this rule even when they do not explicitly state a future behavior of the speaker if such a proposition can be inferred from prior utterances (or from other elements of the context). For example, if P had said "you'll come to see me on Tuesday, won't you," whereupon S had said "absolutely," then S's utterance could be regarded as meeting the propositional content rule for promising because the necessary proposition is recoverable from P's prior utterance. In this case, S could still be heard as promising if the situational (and other) rules are met as well.

For an utterance to be interpreted as a promise, certain conditions about the situation in which it is uttered must hold true so that certain beliefs of the speaker can be inferred. Searle calls these "preparatory conditions" (pp. 58-60), but we shall refer to them as *situational rules*. The first is that there must be sufficient reason for hearers to infer that the speaker believes he or she *is able* to do the future behavior. For example, if S and P had just discussed S's impending trip out of the country beginning on Monday, then P would probably regard S's "then I'll see you Tuesday" as a mistake, a joke (about P coming along on the trip, or about S's trip being extremely short, perhaps), or some other speech act. The utterance would not meet the definition of a promise unless the situation is such that it seems that S believes she actually can see P on Tuesday. A second situational rule is that it must seem that the speaker thinks *the recipient (hearer) wants or is willing for* the speaker's future behavior to be done. This condition captures the characteristic of a promise that the future behavior is regarded as good for the recipient. For example, if S's impending visit to P were for the purpose of collecting a huge overdue loan, S's line 1 might be interpreted as a threat rather than a promise. (Notice, however, that there are some constitutive rules that are common to both promises and threats; more about this later.) In this particular case, P has already said (earlier in the conversation) that he would be available to see students on Tuesday, which is a reason for S to think her proposed visit is okay with him. A third situational rule is that it must seem that the *speaker would not ordinarily do* the future behavior anyway, as a matter of routine. That is, we do not make promises to do things that we routinely do as a matter of course.[7] If S had a standing appointment with P every Tuesday, then line 1 would seem more like a reminder or a way of saying goodbye than a promise. As we shall see, other speech acts have situational rules contributing to their definition, but those rules differ from these three that help define a promise.

In addition to rules having to do with situational conditions, promises (and many other acts) have a sincerity condition.

For an utterance to be interpreted as a valid, proper promise, there must be sufficient reason to infer that the *speaker intends to do* the future behavior. This *sincerity rule* goes beyond the speaker merely believing that he or she is able to do the promised behavior—a promise requires that the speaker actually intends to do it. So if everyone knows that S would not keep her appointment with P (even on a bet!), that she never goes to see her professors (or this particular one), and that she takes great pride in avoiding student-teacher conferences, then S's "I'll see you Tuesday" would probably come off as sarcasm or as a false promise designed to avoid an immediate confrontation with P. In fact, this may be a major reason similar utterances such as "I'll see you later" are usually not interpreted as promises, but rather as goodbyes. What participants know from previous talk and from their daily schedules makes it seem unlikely that the speaker actually intends to make a point of seeing them later. In this particular case, S has earlier asked about when P might be available for a meeting, and it is clearly in her best interest to see P and get the form signed. These are reasons to infer that S is sincere. Valid promises must be sincere.

The final constitutive rule deals with the basic strategic point of a promise: It puts the speaker under an obligation. Searle (1969) calls this the "essential condition." People who share the pragmatic conventions of their language system (for most varieties of English, at least) know that the basic illocutionary point or function of a promise is to create an obligation for the speaker to do the future behavior. We can regard promises, then, as defined by all the constitutive rules discussed up to this point— plus a further one. The *essential rule* is that there is sufficient reason to infer that the speaker intends, by producing the utterance, *to obligate him- or herself* to perform the indicated future behavior. If it seems that the speaker does not intend to undertake such an obligation (as when the ironic "trust me" is used), the utterance will most likely not be interpreted as a valid promise.

So the actual utterance is only one component in the process of interpreting what conversational action is being performed. Under other circumstances, "then I'll see you Tuesday" could amount to the speaker making an offer or even *eliciting* a promise from the hearer.[8] This collective definition of promising that we have discussed in such detail can be further clarified by considering the constitutive rules that define some other speech acts (again, following Searle, pp. 64-71).

The request. Just as an utterance that conveys a promise is about something, so an utterance must be about something in order to meet the definition of requesting. But a request is about a future behavior *of the recipient (the hearer)*, rather than of the speaker. Thus one difference between the speech acts of requesting and promising lies in the propositional content rule. In Data Segment 2.4, J and T (and other participants) are composing a test for a small group communication course. In line 1, J reads a proposed question.

(2.4) [Aakhus, 1988, Testmake 035, p. 65]
1 J: A system is an observable characteristic or dimension of
2   any phenomenon . . . which can change from time to time
3   (1.1)
4 T: Read that one more time.
5 J: A system is an observable characteristic . . . .

In line 4, T requests that the question be repeated. Notice that we hear this request as being addressed to J (who read the question the first time), and thus we hear the propositional content of T's utterance as relating to a future behavior of J: J will "read [the question] one more time."

The situational rules for a request are somewhat different also. For example, participants must be able to infer that the speaker thinks *the recipient (hearer)* is able (and at least potentially willing) to do the requested behavior. Also, there must be reason to suppose that the speaker believes *the recipient* would not ordinarily do the behavior as a matter of course. Applied to T's utterance in the "test question" segment, these rules state

that the situation must be such that J (and perhaps other participants) can infer that T thinks J is able to repeat the question and also that he would probably not do so without someone requesting it. As we can see, the conditions that define a request are similar to those that define a promise, but different in specific ways (for example, a request is about the hearer's behavior rather than the speaker's). This will be apparent in the sincerity rule as well.

For an utterance to be interpreted as a request, participants must be able to infer that the speaker sincerely *wants the recipient* to do the future behavior. The 1.1-second silence in line 3 above can be seen as an indication that T is experiencing some sort of trouble interpreting or judging the proposed question and probably needs it repeated. On the other hand, if J were making a very embarrassing or demeaning statement about T (instead of reading a test question), T's "read that one more time" might come off as a joking comment or even as a challenge or dare ("say that one more time and I'll . . . "). Such an interpretation is possible because of the unlikelihood that T would actually want J to repeat the derogatory statement. That is, it would seem that T's utterance fails to meet the sincerity rule for requests under these (hypothetical) conditions.

The essential rule for requesting is that the utterance can be seen as the speaker's attempt to get the recipient to do the future behavior. See Levinson (1983, p. 240) for a speaker-oriented list of constitutive conditions applying to requests and warnings. Let us conclude our discussion of these definitional rules by taking a very short look at other selected speech acts.

Threats. It was suggested above that to "promise" to do something that is not wanted by the recipient might be interpreted as a threat. Threats are similar to promises in that both involve the speaker's intention to do the future behavior (sincerity rule) and both may involve the undertaking of an obligation to do it (essential rule). Threats differ from promises in that in a threat participants can see that the speaker believes the future behavior would be harmful for the recipient (a situational rule).

Offers. Like a promise, an offer involves the speaker's intent to perform some future behavior for the recipient, so the propositional content rule, the situational rules, and the sincerity rule would be about the same as for the promise. A notable difference, however, is that the obligation is not created until after the offer is accepted by the recipient. This might be incorporated into our system of conventions by specifying the undertaking of a *conditional* obligation, conditional upon an acceptance by the recipient (perhaps as part of the essential rule).

Commands. Orders or commands are constituted by rules similar to those for the request, except that it must be evident that the speaker has some sort of power or authority over the recipient. An additional situational rule to that effect would be conventional for commands.

Compliments. A real (serious) compliment should have, as part of its definition, the condition that the speaker appears to genuinely like whatever the recipient has done that is the occasion for the compliment (sincerity rule).

Speech acts are the actions of conversation.

Greetings. Since greetings do not have to incorporate statement-like meanings about anything (they do not require a proposition), it would seem that they do not have any propositional content requirements. While "hi," for example, is certainly a linguistic symbol, uttering it does not involve saying anything *about* anything. And, of course, we can do a greeting without speaking at all, by waving a hand or nodding the head. We cannot ordinarily do a promise merely by nodding the head unless the propositional content has been specified by the prior use of language.

In summary, speech acts are the actions of conversation. We can regard them as defined or created by a system of pragmatic language conventions that we have called constitutive rules. Some of these rules deal with the propositional content of the utterance, others specify certain characteristics of the situation, still others deal with the sincerity of the speaker, and so on. Participants use these constitutive rules to *interpret* conversational utterances as being certain speech acts. Participants also *design* their utterances to take advantage of the fact that recipients make use of these definitional rules. Thus the system of conventions serves as both an interpretive resource and a design or production resource for people engaged in everyday conversation. As we have seen, some speech acts seem closely related to each other (such as requests and commands) and others are similar in some ways but also "opposite" in certain respects (such as promises and threats). This suggests that it may be useful to view conversation in terms of classes or families of speech acts as opposed to separate, individual ones. We now turn our attention to that task.

SPEECH ACT FAMILIES

Searle (1979, pp. 12-20) presents a detailed argument for a classification system with five categories of speech acts. The categories are based on the purpose or illocutionary point of each act, so that those that function to put the speaker under some sort of obligation are grouped together in the same category, and so forth. Another distinction that Searle makes in this category system is whether the act operates to model or match the world accurately (whether it is, in some sense, descriptive) or instead operates to change the world to match it (whether it is instrumental). Other speech act theorists have also proposed category systems (for example, see Austin, 1975; Bach & Harnish, 1979), but we will explore the following five families of speech acts based on Searle's analysis.

Commissives. The first speech act that we discussed at length was the promise. The purpose or illocutionary point of a promise is to commit the speaker to some future behavior (the essential rule). We saw that an offer has a similar point (but that the offer has to be accepted before the speaker is committed). Both of these are *commissives.* That is, commissives are those speech acts whose purpose or point is to commit the speaker to some course of action. Such related acts as making a vow, taking a pledge, and giving a guarantee are also in this family, differing from a promise mostly in how formal or official they are. Notice that commissives do not merely *describe* the speaker as being committed; a successful promise or pledge *actually commits* the speaker. It is in this sense that commissives operate to change the world rather than merely to describe it correctly. For example, S's "Okay (1.0) then I'll see you Tuesday" (Segment 2.3, above) changes S's relationship toward her conversational partner and toward a future behavior: She is now committed to seeing P. Commissives, through a set of pragmatic language conventions, create a state of commitment between the speaker and one or more other participants. Of course, speakers do more than commit themselves to perform future behaviors (or not to perform them, as in the case of a promise not to do something); they also attempt to get others to perform such behaviors. To do this they employ another family of speech acts.

Directives. The purpose or point of all *directives* is to get the recipient to do something. Requests, such as "Read that one more time," are typical directives. Searle (1979, pp. 13-14) notes that the strength of the speaker's attempt to get another participant to perform some behavior varies from one directive to another, so this category includes very strong, official, and insistent acts such as commands and orders, but it also includes milder ones such as suggestions and giving permission. Questions designed to get answers from another participant are directives in the sense that they are attempts to get someone to talk about something. Keep in mind that the term *question* here names a speech act, not merely an interrogative sentence. As in the case of commissives, directives operate on the world to make it more like the propositional content of the utterance. "Read that one more time," spoken by T (Segment 2.4) is an attempt to get J to change his behavior to make it fit this proposition: J read(s) that (test question) one more time. So this characteristic that the words are meant to change the world is common to both commissives and directives. Not all speech acts have this characteristic, however, and we next examine the category in which the "direction of fit" (Searle's term) is the opposite—the words are supposed to match or fit the way the world is, rather than change it.

Assertives. Back in the "sandwich" episode (Segment 2.1), B offered K part of her sandwich by saying "Are you sure that you don't want half?" As discussed above, that offer is a commissive. But B also did something else (in line 5)—she described the sandwich: "This is huge." That is, B asserted a particular characteristic of the sandwich. Notice that this description does not operate to change the sandwich at all (although it does seem to encourage K to accept B's offer, a matter we will consider later). Instead, the connection between the description and the world is that the talk ought to describe the world accurately. The purpose or point of *assertives* is to display the speaker's belief in the propositional content of the utterance. Whatever the conventional meaning of "huge" might be for these participants, B has displayed her belief in the proposition: "This [sandwich] is huge." So when we describe something, we are interpreted as proposing that the description is a correct one; when we claim that a certain thing is the case, we are seen as sincerely believing that it is in fact the case, and so on. The category of assertives includes such speech acts as statements, descriptions, and assertions (but there is no suggestion whatever that the speaker is being "assertive" or aggressive). It also includes those acts in which the speaker limits his or her degree of certainty about the matter, such as predicting or speculating about something. But given the varying degrees of confidence that a speaker might display about the truth of the proposition being asserted, the sincerity rule for assertives is nevertheless that the speaker can be seen as having the appropriate belief in that truth. So whereas a commissive can be judged as insincere (it seems that the speaker does not intend to perform), and a directive can also be judged as insincere (it seems the speaker does not want the recipient to perform), an assertive is heard as sincere when it seems that the speaker believes its proposition is true (and insincere when it seems he or she believes it is false). But what about "statements" such as "Oh it was just beautiful," in Segment 2.2? We said that A was giving B a compliment, and it seems that A's utterance is more an expression of her feelings than an assertion of objective fact about "it." This compliment is not an assertive at all, but a member of a fourth family of speech acts.

Expressives. Compliments, apologies, welcomes, and thanks all have in common that they are expressions of the speaker's psychological state about something (an event, an object, a behavior, or whatever) that has to do with either the speaker or the recipient. These speech acts are *expressives.* Their sincerity condition is that recipients can infer that the speaker actually does have the psychological state expressed (in the case of compliments, being pleased about something the recipient has done; in the case of apologies, being sorry for something the speaker has done; and so on). As for what it is that the psychological state relates to (e.g., the "it" in A's "Oh it was just beautiful"), notice that these events, objects, and so on are taken for granted in expressives. So the expressive does not operate either to change the world or to represent it accurately, but rather presupposes the way the world is and expresses the speaker's psychological state about it. Consider Data Segment 2.5, in which a student and his spouse are moving to another state; a professor (N) is saying goodbye (on the phone) to the student.

(2.5) [field notes]
 1 N: Well listen. You folks have a good trip back.
 2 M: Yeh. Thank you.

If we interpret line 1 as wishing or bidding the travelers a good trip, as opposed to urging them to take steps to have a good trip (in which case this would be a directive rather than an expressive), then the point of the act is to express the speaker's wish. The situation described in the propositional content of the utterance is assumed: "You folks [will] have a good trip." One subset of the category of expressives includes acts that seem to be expressions of some state (perhaps a psychological one) but that do not seem to have any propositional content. The speech acts of greeting a person and acknowledging a participant's utterance (by saying "uh huh" or something similar) are cases in point. Bach and Harnish (1979) highlight these nonpropositional utterances by calling the entire category "acknowledgments," including essentially what Searle calls expressives. So we will regard the family of expressives as including certain more or less ritual speech acts (cousins, as it were) that acknowledge the presence, departure, or conversational actions of other participants. It might seem that the four categories we have discussed thus far cover all the important types of conversational speech acts, but Searle (1979) argues that it is useful to have a category for those more or less *official* actions that occur in the context of some institution, organization, or government. An example would be a judge sentencing someone to jail.

Declarations. When a properly authorized speaker performs a *declaration* under the proper conditions (as defined not only by pragmatic language conventions, but also by the rules of the particular institution involved), such a "successful performance guarantees that the propositional content corresponds to the world" (Searle, 1979, p. 17). Saying it actually makes it so! When the boss (under the proper circumstances) tells an employee, "You're fired," that employee is *thereby* fired. When the boss says to an employee,

> *Certain speech acts are similar in that they have a similar point or function in the conversational "game."*

"I am appointing you as chairperson of the appeals committee," the boss is not merely describing the appointment, but rather actually making the appointment via that utterance. When the judge tells a convicted defendant, "I sentence you to thirty days in the county jail," the defendant is thereby sentenced to jail for thirty days. Granted, these official acts are not the common fare of ordinary conversation, but their status as actions performed through talk is clear.

In summary, the definitions of speech acts (the constitutive rules) make it possible for us to group together various conversational actions for analytical and practical purposes. We can see that certain speech acts are similar in that they have a similar point or function in a given conversational "game." Those in the family of directives all function in some way to get the recipient to do something; those that we classify as assertives convey information about how the speaker sees the world; commissives function to commit the speaker to do something; expressives function to express the speaker's feelings or to acknowledge the recipient in some way; and so on. It is vitally important as we conduct conversation to understand correctly which categories of speech acts the participants are using. For example, what sort of conversational action is being produced when "I love you" is uttered? If it is an expressive (sincerely performed), then we know something of how the speaker feels. But does that utterance function at all as a commissive? Is the speaker making any sort of commitments about his or her future behavior? And think about this possibility: Could the speaker be using "I love you" primarily as a directive, as an attempt to get the recipient to perform some behavior? Another application of this system of categorizing speech acts might arise when we find that a particular speech act is too forceful or not forceful enough for our purposes. We know that we can switch to another act from the same family category (choosing among command, request, and suggestion, for example) and still get the communicative job done. Or we might vary the actual wording of the utterance so as to focus attention on one thing rather than another without changing the basic point of our action. For example, recipients of a compliment might find it less awkward to respond if the compliment is worded as a proposition about the speaker's feelings ("I'm fascinated by your idea") rather than as a proposition about the recipient ("Your idea is so fascinating"). Yet each of these utterances, under the proper conditions, comes off as an expressive with compliment characteristics. Such issues raise some questions about speech acts that our discussion thus far has not answered, questions such as how a speaker can be taken to mean something that he or she has not actually said, or how an utterance that does not literally direct or commit (for example) can be routinely interpreted as a directive or commissive.

COMPLICATIONS FOR SPEECH ACT THEORY

What is gained by looking at conversation in terms of speech act theory and what are the primary shortcomings of such an approach? Analyzing the constitutive rules that define conversational actions reveals for us the importance and pervasiveness of certain kinds of assumptions or expectations in everyday talk. In interpreting an utterance as a particular speech act, participants rely on shared conventions about what speakers are expected to believe, want, intend, and so on. Speech act theory describes those conventional assumptions in an orderly way and thus reveals important similarities and differences among various conversational actions. Speech act theory also illuminates the difference between the propositional (linguistic) meaning of an utterance and its status as an action. This is a critical distinction in our understanding the conduct of conversation. But speech act theory is not by any means a perfect tool for achieving that understanding. Much happens in conversation that is not satisfactorily explained by appealing to constitutive rules and speech acts—or, at least, that can be equally well explained by using other analytical schemes.

One problem is that speech act theory tends to overestimate the prevalence of conventional (rule-defined) meaning in conversation and to underestimate the extent of meaning that goes beyond what has been said in so many words (or is even contradictory to it). Participants routinely construct meanings that fill in or expand the meaning of what someone actually said. In Data Segment 2.6, for example, Y and her son Aaron are on the verge of moving across the country and are attending a farewell dinner given by friends. Y is telling her dinner companions about an event that happened at her son's place of employment. Note the start and end of overlapping talk indicated by brackets between the lines.

(2.6) [Farewell Dinner]
```
 8  Y:  T'day was Aaron's last day at McDonald's land ┌(.)   ┐and
 9  J:                                                 └Oh::  ┘
10  Y:  they gave him a cake=
11  ( ):  =(┌  )
12  R:      └Oh did they: (0.8) great.
```

The rest of the participants (J, R, and the unknown speaker in line 11) heard Y as meaning that "they" gave Aaron a cake *because* it was his last day, although Y does not explicitly say so. In addition, the participants understood that "T'day" was

Aaron's last day at work *because of his moving away*, although neither Y nor anyone else in the conversation actually said that either. So Y is treated as having made assertions that she did not make; she probably even counted on the other participants' constructing such additional meanings. A related occurrence is when participants interpret an utterance as being an additional or even different speech act from what it would seem to be from the utterance alone. Under some circumstances, Y could have been interpreted as excusing Aaron's failure to eat the proper amount of food at dinner (because he ate too much cake earlier). An excuse might be an expressive. At the same time, Y would still be seen as stating or asserting the information about what happened earlier in the day (an assertive). In the "compliment" example (Data Segment 2.2), A's "Oh it was just <u>beautiful</u>" could be interpreted sarcastically in the right situation and taken to mean that "it" was horrible.

Notice how these altered examples appeal to circumstances and situations. This suggests that we ought to give the conversational context of an utterance even more importance than speech act theory does, through its situational and other rules. It is also important to note that the three conventional types of sentences—declarative, interrogative, and imperative—are frequently not used to produce the categories of speech acts that we might expect. Levinson (1983, p. 275) reminds us, for example, that studies have shown that imperatives are more likely to be used in directions, instructions, wishes ("have a good trip back"), invitations ("come to the movies with me"), welcomings ("come on in"), and so on than in requests or commands. What is needed to further our understanding of these conversational phenomena is a perspective that focuses on how participants calculate, infer, or otherwise "arrive at" meanings using conventional meaning as one resource in the interpretation. Although there are several such schemes available, we will primarily consider the one devised by Grice (1975).

❏ Interpretive Foundations

In one sense, even conventionally derived meanings are constructed through a process of interpretation. A whole range of
information, besides the utterance itself, has to be taken into
account by participants in order to identify the conversational
action being produced. We have discussed some of these considerations above, but remember that we made no claim that
they are processed consciously, or that participants are necessarily aware of what leads them to interpret a given utterance
as a particular speech act. They may or may not be aware.

In another sense, however, participants seem to engage in
processes of interpretation that go beyond conventionally derived meanings. We routinely interpret speakers in conversation as meaning more than—or something different from—the
conventional meanings of their utterances. For this reason, we
will refer to these latter processes (even though they may involve some conventions) as the *interpretive foundations* of conversational action. In particular, we shall now examine a system
of interpretation through which speakers are said to convey
meanings beyond the literal meanings of their words.

CONVERSATIONAL IMPLICATURE

Grice (1975, 1978) has proposed a theory in which a limited
set of conversational principles may be used by participants,
along with characteristics of the situation and the immediate
conversational context, to construct inferences about what a
speaker means. From the speaker's point of view, designing an
utterance to require the use of these principles for its interpretation is said to *implicate* a meaning. The term *implicate* is used
rather than *imply* to remind us that the process does not necessarily follow the rules of formal logic. Accordingly, Grice's
system is a theory of *conversational implicature*. He begins with
a very general principle that directs participants to design their

"Can you pass the salt?"

utterances to fulfill the immediate requirements of the conversational episode. This is the *cooperative principle,* which we can
paraphrase this way: Cooperate with your conversational partners; make your talk do just what is needed at the moment you
utter it. Grice (1975) then proposes several more specific principles, called *maxims,* that together amount to the cooperative
principle. If we follow all the maxims, then we are being cooperative. Some of these maxims contain more than one idea, and
an especially clear description of them is provided by Geis
(1982); we will use his version of the maxims (p. 31).

   The maxims. Part of the cooperative principle has to do with
how much a speaker says. This can be represented by two
maxims. The *maxim of strength* requires us to "say no less than
is necessary" or, more positively: Say enough! Its counterpart
is the *maxim of parsimony:* "Say no more than is necessary." In
other words, don't say too much! We can see how these two

maxims might apply in conversation by imagining that we have
proposed a test question (to a group that has the task of creating
an exam), just as J did back in Data Segment 2.4. Imagine further
that another participant then requests that we "read that one
more time" (as T did). Now, according to the maxim of strength,
we should repeat the entire question, or at least the part of it
that we think is causing the other person trouble; perhaps we
should even add a few words of clarification. To say less than
that would be to say less than is necessary for immediate
communicative purposes. And according to the maxim of parsimony we ought to repeat only the question itself and not the
part of our utterance that introduced the question (for example,
"Okay, I have one more question from chapter twelve, so here
goes"). Since it is the wording of the question itself that seems
to be causing the problem, to repeat other parts of the utterance would be to say more than is necessary. So part of making
one's conversational contribution just what is needed at the
moment is to say the appropriate quantity: Make the message
informative enough (strength), but also as economical as possible (parsimony).

Another part of the cooperative principle has to do with the
quality of what one says. Again, two maxims conveniently
represent this concern. The *maxim of truth* enjoins: "Do not say
anything that you believe to be false." In other words, don't lie!
Its companion is the *maxim of evidence*: "Do not say anything
for which you lack adequate evidence." The distinction between the two can be illustrated by considering Y's assertion
(in the "cake" example) about her son being given a cake on his
last day at work. If Y knew that no such farewell ceremony had
taken place (if, for example, her son had reported that his final
day at work had been routine), then her utterance in lines 8
and 10 would have been a violation of the maxim of truth. But
suppose that she had no idea what sort of day her son's last
day at work had been; suppose that she had not talked to her
son at all since he finished work. In that case, she would not be
lying in the strict sense of the term, since she would not actually
know that her utterance made a false claim. But she would be

violating the maxim of evidence by saying something about which she had no knowledge. In adhering to the cooperative principle, then, we must see to it that our talk is of good quality as well as of appropriate quantity.

An important consideration in following the cooperative principle is to make our contribution relevant to the conversation in some way. We can state the *maxim of relevance* simply: "Be relevant." What exactly that might mean in practice is not a simple matter, however. There are many ways in which an utterance might be relevant at some specific point in the conversation. It could be relevant to the overall goal(s) of the participants, to the immediate topic or theme, to the immediate health or safety of the participants, or to some event that happens during the progress of the conversation. In Data Segment 2.7 (which is later in the B-K conversation than we saw in Segment 2.1), the participants are talking about going home for Christmas.

(2.7) [Craig & Tracy, 1983a, B-K, p. 305, simplified]
39 K: Oh where's your mom living.
        ((pause))
40 B: ((laugh))=
41 K: =You weren't supposed to take a bite right then.
        ((pause))
42 B: My mother lives in Minneapolis.

In utterance 41, K comments on B's inability to answer the question in utterance 39 because of B's just having taken a bite of food. Thus K's utterance is relevant even though it is not about visiting relatives at Christmas. And B's utterance 42 is relevant because it is about the issue of visiting relatives and is specifically an answer to K's question in 39. As we shall see, the maxim of relevance has especially wide scope.

Finally, following the cooperative principle involves the manner in which we speak. In particular, the clarity of the language we use is important. The *maxim of clarity* instructs us to avoid language that is unfamiliar to the recipient(s). A violation of that maxim (for most everyday audiences) would occur if we instructed a speaker or writer to "eschew obfuscation." That means about the same thing as "avoid unfamiliar language," but most people would not understand it. So we must be clear as well as truthful, relevant, sufficiently informative, and so on, if we are to comply fully with the cooperative principle.

It seems that participants overwhelmingly do comply with the cooperative principle. And we ordinarily assume that our conversational partners are intending to cooperate unless we have repeated evidence to the contrary. But do people consistently follow each of the maxims? When we tell jokes or stories, for example, it seems that we often ignore the maxims of truth and evidence. And if our purpose is to maintain friendly chit-chat while we wait for some event to take place, we often seem to violate the maxim of parsimony. In fact, it seems that these six maxims taken together apply primarily to serious, information-oriented conversation. The many other kinds of language games that we engage in do not seem to require adherence to all of the maxims in order for one to be a cooperative participant. Just how valid for ordinary conversation is this theory of Grice and others?

Implicature. In discussing the conventions that define speech acts, we introduced a distinction between constitutive rules (which we then examined in some detail) and regulative rules. Constitutive rules define—actually create the possibility of—a particular speech act, while regulative rules specify when and where the speech act must or must not be employed. Our discussion of the cooperative principle and its maxims has portrayed them as very general, widely applicable regulative rules. Notice how we have described participants as "adhering to" the cooperative principle and the maxims. We have said that the maxims "require," "enjoin," and "instruct" participants to converse in certain ways. These are terms of regulation and, indeed, all the maxims are usually expressed as regulative rules (be relevant, do not lie, be clear, and so on). See Shimanoff

(1980) for an extensive discussion of regulative rules. But while
it may be open to question how widely people follow these
maxims in conversation, it is not pri-
marily the *regulative* function of the
cooperative principle and its maxims
that is at issue here. Grice's reason for
proposing these maxims is not to show
that people's talk is tightly regulated
by them, but rather to show how people use them in *interpreting the meaning*
of that talk.

*Everyone assumes
that participants
are trying to follow
the cooperative
principle.*

The basic idea of conversational im-
plicature is that everyone *assumes* that participants are trying to
follow the cooperative principle and its maxims. When a recipient is faced with an utterance that seems to fall short of com-
pletely meeting the requirements of the maxims, he or she fills
in or alters the conventional meaning of that utterance so that
it does meet those requirements. That is, the recipient constructs an interpretation that *preserves the assumption* that the
speaker really is being cooperative and is following the maxims. Speakers design their utterances so as to leave room for
this added or altered meaning; they rely on their recipients'
ability to make these nonconventional interpretations. Let us
see how this might work in specific instances.

In the "cake" example (Data Segment 2.6), Y says that today
was her son's "last day at McDonald's land (.) and they gave
him a <u>cake</u>." We have already noted that recipients interpret this
utterance as meaning that the cake was given because it was
Aaron's last day at work and because he was moving away,
even though this was not actually said. Y implicates those
meanings rather than conveying them directly. The implicature
and the resulting interpretation by the other participants work
something like this: (a) Y has said that "they" gave Aaron a cake,
but she has not said why; (b) since Y has stressed the word *cake*,
and since giving a cake is something of a special occasion
anyway, Y should tell us why the cake was given if she is
following the maxim of strength; (c) but we *assume* that Y *is*

following the cooperative principle and its maxims, there being no serious evidence to the contrary; (d) therefore, Y must think that we are able to figure out why the cake was given, perhaps by combining what she has said with something that we know; (e) we all know that Y and Aaron are moving away and that his coworkers probably know this, and Y knows that we know; (f) therefore, since an obvious reason to give Aaron a cake would be that he is moving away, Y must intend for us to conclude that that is what she means. Thus, by seeming not to give quite enough information, Y implicates additional meaning and we interpret her as adhering to the maxim of strength after all.

If B, in the "going home for Christmas" example (Segment 2.7), had answered K's "Oh where's your mom living" by saying "my mother lives about a ten-minute taxi ride from the Minneapolis airport," B might well have been interpreted as implicating something beyond the mere facts of her mother's location. At this point in the conversation, only the name of a city is needed to meet the immediate communicative demands. But rather than find B in violation of the maxim of parsimony (saying too much), participants are more likely to interpret her as intending to convey something different, such as that her mother is very conveniently located for a visit. Thus B would be interpreted not as giving extraneous details, but rather as implicating the ease with which her mother can be visited, and as adhering to the maxim of parsimony.

The system of implicature can operate even when the speaker flagrantly and obviously violates a maxim. Consider another hypothetical variation of B's response in that same example: "My mother lives in Katmandu." In the context of a discussion about going home for Christmas, and given that both participants know that B's mother does not live in Nepal, but rather lives somewhere in the midwestern United States, such an utterance would likely not be regarded by K as an outrageous lie on B's part. Even though B has clearly violated the maxim of truth, K would probably preserve the assumption that B really is being cooperative and would give the utterance a different interpretation. Here is one possibility: B is implicating that her mother lives in a place that is out of reach for a Christmas visit. So in this case, the speaker is interpreted as meaning something quite different from what she actually said, as following the cooperative principle after all, but as exploiting the maxim of truth to achieve this special implicature.

The other maxims can serve as resources in conversational implicature as well, and the maxim of relevance is an especially rich source of implicatures. Geis (1982, pp. 50-53) discusses several advertising claims that involve implicatures based on this maxim. For an example from conversation, consider Data Segment 2.8, in which a boy of about 12 (S) is trying to sell a newspaper subscription to a man (R).

(2.8) [Jefferson & Schenkein, 1978, p. 156]
11 S: G'n aftuhnoon sir, W'dju be innerested in subscribing
12   to the Progress Bulletin t'help m'win a trip tuh Cape
13   Kennedy to see the astronauts on the moon shot. . . .
17 R: Well I <u>live</u> in Los Angeles. I don'live around here but
18   <u>these</u> fellas live here, you might- ask the:m, I don'
19   <u>know</u>

Apparently, S interprets R's utterance in lines 17-19 as a "no" answer, because S immediately begins asking the other people present if they want to subscribe. We also interpret R as meaning no, even though he did not actually say "no." How does this implicature work? A close inspection of R's utterance shows that it might be considered a violation of the maxim of relevance, coming as it does after S's solicitation. What S needs from R is a yes or no response, but R says "Well I <u>live</u> in Los Angeles . . . ." If we (and the participants) assume that R intends his utterance to be relevant, however, then we can search for and find a connection between R's stated place of residence and the answer that S needs. In this case, that connection is the everyday knowledge that people subscribe to newspapers in their local neighborhoods—not from across town or from a different city. R relies on his recipient(s) to work out that the answer to S's solicitation is a no by using this knowledge and

R's statement that he does not live locally. We thus interpret the speaker as implicating a proper answer to S after all by preserving our assumption that he is being relevant. Again, this mechanism seems to work even when the speaker flagrantly violates the maxim. For example, an answer such as "Is the pope Catholic?" is usually quite irrelevant to the topic of the yes-no question it follows. But by assuming that the speaker really is being cooperative, we can interpret such an utterance as a way of displaying a yes answer. See Nofsinger (1976) for further discussion of this sort of answering technique.

This theory of conversational implicature is an attempt to explain, using general principles of human rationality and general maxims of conversational conduct, how it is that participants can say one thing and yet be interpreted as meaning something more, or even something quite different. But what does implicature have to do with conversational *action*? It seems, for example, that the difference between saying "my mother lives in Minneapolis" and "my mother lives in Katmandu" is a difference in propositional content rather than a difference in speech acts. Both of those utterances are statements or assertions. It turns out, however, that implicature is one way of explaining how a speaker can produce an utterance that, if taken literally, would seem to count as one speech act and yet be interpreted as having done an additional or even quite different speech act. This is a very common occurrence in conversation and is known (in speech act theory) as the problem of indirect speech acts.

INDIRECT SPEECH ACTS

We saw in the "newspaper" example (Data Segment 2.8) that S solicits a newspaper subscription from R and that R replies with a statement about where he lives. But R's utterance comes off not primarily as a statement at all, but as a refusal or rejection of S's solicitation. S's utterance is a type of directive (an attempt to get R to subscribe) that has much in common with

requests. R declines by producing an utterance that is designed like a statement (a type of assertive) but functions as a
rejection. Bach and Harnish (1979, pp. 51-
55) put rejections in the category we have
called expressives (which they call acknowledgments). So while R has directly
(literally) done a statement, he has indirectly done a rejection—two speech acts
that are not even in the same general category. The problem for speech act theory
is to explain how utterances can be inter-
preted as *indirect speech acts*. One possible solution is the process
of conversational implicature. We discussed above how R's
utterance can be interpreted as meaning no. We can now change
terminology and describe the process in terms of speech acts
rather than linguistic or propositional meaning. What S needs
from R is an acceptance or a rejection of the solicitation. R has
produced an utterance that, if interpreted literally, fails to meet
this need; it is a statement. If we assume that R intends his
utterance to be relevant, however, then we can find a connection between the utterance and the type of speech act that is
needed at the moment. As discussed above, the common practice of subscribing to newspapers where we live rather than
elsewhere connects the utterance to a rejection of the solicitation. Since that speech act is of a type that fulfills the communicative requirements, while a mere statement does not, the
utterance is interpreted as a rejection.

> *Being indirect*
> *is one important*
> *way of being*
> *polite or tactful.*

Just to illustrate how subtle and unnoticed indirect speech
acts can be, let us examine S's utterance about the newspaper
subscription more carefully. Notice that S does not directly say
anything like "please subscribe to the Progress Bulletin." What
S actually says is "W'dju be innerested in subscribing." That is,
S seems most directly to have asked an informational question
of R: Would you be interested? But we (and the participants)
sense that S is not merely seeking information. Notice how odd
it would be if the participants treated it that way: "Are you

interested in subscribing?" "Yes, I'm interested." "Just won-dered" (and S leaves without getting the subscription). Our interpretation is that S really intends to do a solicitation, a request for R to subscribe, but does it indirectly. In fact, being indirect is one important way of being polite or tactful in conversation (Brown & Levinson, 1978), so in many circum-stances, indirect speech acts are routinely used instead of their more direct counterparts. "Would you like to see a movie" is used as an invitation, not merely as a question about the recipient's likes. "Can you pass the casserole" is normally used as a request to pass it, not merely as a question about the recipient's ability (although if the casserole were very heavy, the utterance might be interpreted as both a question and a request). It almost seems that if an utterance makes reference to the recipient's ability, interest, or willingness to perform some future behavior, or to the speaker's desire that the recipient do it (precisely those conditions mentioned in the situational and sincerity rules that define requests), the utterance will be inter-preted as an indirect request. Jacobs and Jackson (1983b) argue that this is because "people are goal-oriented and often try to understand remarks by searching for their relevance to plans for practical actions" (p. 299). In fact, Jacobs and Jackson pro-pose a continuum of directives ranging from direct requests, through indirect requests based on inferential processes such as implicature, to even more veiled requestlike speech acts based on what precedes or follows in the conversation. In Chapter 3 we shall take up some alternative explanations of the workings of indirect speech acts. In order to do this, we will have to examine more closely the context in which utterances are inter-preted as conversational actions.

❏ The Context of Action

Both speech act theory and conversational implicature theory incorporate elements of the context in which talk takes place.

Speech act theory posits constitutive rules that specify how certain aspects of context help to define particular speech acts (the situational rules are examples of this). Implicature theory posits that when context shows the literal interpretation of an utterance to be an implausible violation of the cooperative principle and its maxims, an indirect or implicated interpretation is made instead. So these treatments of conversational action do attempt to take context into account. But an utterance's context—especially the talk that immediately surrounds the utterance—plays an even more intricate and vital role than the speech act and implicature perspectives suggest. Some analysts of everyday conversation argue that the exact meaning of an utterance cannot be known apart from the context in which it is produced, a characteristic of language they call *indexicality* (Leiter, 1980, pp. 107-116). To say that an utterance is indexical is to say that it serves as an index, a sort of pointer, to certain aspects of its context. Participants find those aspects of the context and use them to make a specific interpretation of the utterance. Notice that this view gives the primary role in establishing the speech act meaning of an utterance to participants' interpretive processes and to elements of the immediate context (rather than to convention). There can be no doubt that the talk that occurs along with any given utterance plays a profound role in the interpretation of that utterance. One of the major weaknesses of speech act theory is that it tends to conceptualize speech acts as separate, individual actions, rather than as integrated components in the ongoing flow of conversation. We can begin to correct this shortcoming by recognizing that many conversational actions seem to occur in pairs (or, at least, participants expect them to occur in pairs). A greeting is usually paired with another greeting, a question with an answer, and so on. The importance of this in the interpretation of conversational action cannot be overestimated: It is in the very next speaker's turn that we can see how a given utterance has been interpreted and treated (Heritage, 1984b, p. 245).

❑ Summary

The conduct of conversation involves the participants' production of utterances (linguistically meaningful messages). People employ these utterances in order to produce speech acts (social or communicative actions). Each particular speech act is defined by a set of conventions (constitutive rules) specifying the intent of the speaker, the beliefs that the speaker has about the situation, the propositional content of the utterance, and the like. From the recipient's (hearer's) point of view, these conventions specify what recipients must perceive the speaker's intentions and beliefs to be in order to interpret a given utterance as a particular speech act. Conversational interaction displays a wide variety of speech acts with many different shadings and nuances, but they can be grouped together for analytical purposes into four categories: commissives, directives, assertives, and expressives (with a fifth category, declarations, for more formal or official actions). A particularly fascinating feature of conversation is that people can say one thing and have some confidence that other participants will interpret them as meaning something else. An act that results from saying something different from the conventional, literal way of producing that act is said to be an indirect speech act. One way of explaining how this process works involves a system of conversational implicature by which participants lead each other to attribute meaning that is different from (or in addition to) the conventional meaning an utterance might convey. This system is based on general principles of conversational behavior (the cooperative principle and its maxims) and on the interpretations that result from apparent violations of those principles. But conversational speech acts do not occur in isolation. One of the most powerful factors affecting how participants interpret an utterance—especially what action they take it to be—is the utterance's location in a sequence of other conversational actions. Consequently, in Chapter 3 we shall give extended treatment to pairs of actions and to the various uses to which such sequences of actions can be put. Thus we will extend our focus on the actions of conversation to the *exchange* of actions and the interactive structures that result.

❑ Notes

1. Throughout Chapter 2 and subsequent chapters, refer to the Appendix for an explanation of the special symbols used in the data segments. The "B-K conversation" involves a "make-talk" situation in which two women college students who were acquainted with each other talked together for about a half an hour so that they could be recorded.

2. In Levinson's (1983) words, the distinction is that "a sentence is an abstract theoretical entity defined within a theory of grammar, while an utterance is the issuance of a sentence, a sentence-analogue, or sentence-fragment, in an actual context" (p. 18).

3. Austin presented his ideas on speech acts in 1955 as the William James Lectures at Harvard University. His notes were edited and published after his death.

4. While Searle and most other speech act theorists focus primarily on defining illocutionary acts from the *speaker's* point of view, we shall attempt to adjust the constitutive rules to fit the perspective of the *hearer*—those recipients who have to make an interpretation of what speech act any given utterance amounts to.

5. Conditions such as these had been earlier termed *felicity conditions* by Austin, and that term is frequently used in writings in pragmatics. I have used the term *situational conditions* in place of Searle's *preparatory conditions* because I think it will be more comfortable for readers from a communication background.

6. Two utterances directed at P by a third participant, one that overlaps S's line 1 and one that overlaps the end of S's line 3, have been omitted as not relevant to the conversational actions that S and P are performing. Data segment citations not listed in the references are from my own resources.

7. This, perhaps, explains the unhappy feeling that a person would experience if his or her spouse were suddenly to "promise" to remain faithful. We can imagine that this would not be a reassuring action, in part because it suggests (and reveals) that the spouse has not routinely been faithful in the past.

8. Thanks to Claudia L. Hale for the "elicit a promise" insight.

3

Action Sequences

Virtually every conversational action occurs in a sequence of other conversational actions. An utterance's position within such a sequence has a very powerful influence on how it will be interpreted. It is vital to an effective understanding of the conduct of conversation that we thoroughly explore how participants use their sense of prior talk in conveying a particular action. Detailed examination of talk in a variety of settings by conversation analysts has demonstrated that participants design or "shape" their utterances so as to fit with what has just been said, as well as what they anticipate might be said later. They also design their utterances so as to take into account who is talking to whom and why, what the intended recipients probably know, what they have just said, and so on. As Motley (1990) has discussed, linguistic communication is thoroughly other-directed. This *shaping* of utterances to fit the needs and backgrounds of the participants who will likely interpret those utterances is called *recipient design*. When we use this term, we do not necessarily mean that the speaker is consciously aware of the details of his or her talk, or that the shape of that talk was planned in advance, although either of these could be true in any given case. When we discuss the "design" of an utterance, we mean only that it does have some particular design or shape (just as we can talk about the design of a snowflake without implying that anyone planned it).

> *An utterance counts as some particular action not only because of what it says, but because of the talk that surrounds it.*

We mentioned at the end of Chapter 2 that many (though not all) conversational actions tend to occur in pairs. Participants often exchange greetings, for example, so that a greeting is followed by another greeting (the same is true of goodbyes), and questions are followed by answers. In this chapter, we will examine the paired nature of such actions. We will also see how participants combine pairs (and other groupings) of actions into longer stretches of talk to accomplish the work of the conversation. Our approach will be quite different from the perspective we used in Chapter 2, however. There, we focused on the intuitions of language users (their "sense" of what makes a promise, for example) and on the conventions they use to define speech acts; our purpose was to stimulate thinking about conversation as action. But conversation is not merely a collection of actions—it is a process of *inter*action. An utterance counts as some particular action not only because of what it says, what the speaker intends, and so on, but because of the talk that surrounds it. That is, the way an utterance is interpreted (and the way it is designed) depends overwhelmingly on where it is located in a sequence of actions. Think, for example, about such utterances as "Is the pope Catholic?" ("Do birds fly?" and so on). Such an utterance counts as a yes answer when it follows a yes/no question. In other conversational locations, it could be interpreted as a request for information. Accordingly, in this chapter we focus on the *structures* that participants assemble and how those structures influence the interpretation of conversational action. We begin with a look at those actions that seem to occur in pairs and seem somehow incomplete when they do not.

❑ Adjacency Pairs

We noted that greetings and goodbyes usually occur two at a time, and we might well have added insults, wishes ("Have a nice day"), and a few others. Many other actions are also typically paired, but with a different type of action rather than with the same type. For example, invitations are typically followed by acceptances (or rejections of some sort), congratulations by thanks, accusations by apologies (or denials), offers by acceptances (or refusals), and so on. As we shall see, when one of these first actions has been produced, participants orient to the presence or absence of the relevant second action. There is an expectation by participants that the second action should be produced, and when it does not occur, participants behave as if it should have. So the idea of action pairs will be useful in understanding the conduct of conversation.

One of the most powerful concepts we have for understanding conversation is the idea of the *adjacency pair*. Schegloff and Sacks (1973) propose this concept as a way to discuss paired actions. An adjacency pair has the following characteristics: (a) It is a sequence of two communicative actions; (b) the two actions often occur adjacent to each other; (c) they are produced by different speakers; (d) one action is a *first pair part* and the other is a *second pair part*, that is, they are sequentially ordered; and (e) they are categorized or type-connected so that any given first pair part must be matched with one of a relatively few types of second pair parts.[1] For example, consider Data Segment 3.1, in which B is suggesting an alternative arrangement after having just rejected E's offer of lunch.

(3.1) [field notes]
1 B: W'll maybe we ought tuh think about goin' out
2   an havin' a bite tuh eat this <u>eve</u>ning.
3   (.)
4 E: O::kay

Here we have two actions: B's invitation or suggestion in lines
1-2 and E's acceptance in line 4. The two actions are adjacent
(no other talk comes between them) and they are produced by
two different speakers. The actions are ordered, the invitation
being a first pair part and the acceptance being a second pair
part. (Notice that reversing them, "O::kay," "W'll maybe we
ought tuh . . . " still gives the impression that "okay" is a second
pair part to some unknown, prior utterance; and we still expect
the invitation to be answered.) Invitations belong to a category
of action that is paired primarily with the categories of acceptance and rejection, and in this case, the invitation gets an
acceptance. So these two actions fit together in the special way
outlined above, and together they form a basic conversational
structure—an adjacency pair.

Although not all segments of conversation are composed of
adjacency pairs, some segments are built by stringing several
adjacency pairs together. One place where this occurs fairly
commonly is in the opening of telephone conversations, as in
Data Segment 3.2.

(3.2) [Schegloff, 1979, p. 55]
1   ((telephone presumably rings))
2 H: H'llo:?
3 R: Harriet?
4 H: Yeah?
5 R: Hi!
6 H: Hi:.

We can see that (at least) two sorts of things are done in this
segment: identification work and greeting work. In line 3, R's
utterance is a special type of question that Schegloff (1979) calls
a "confirmation request" (pp. 48-49). R, who is the caller in this

case, essentially asks the answerer (H) to confirm that she is Harriet. Just as a question is paired with an answer, this confirmation request is the first pair part of an adjacency pair that takes a confirmation or disconfirmation as the second pair part. In line 4, H provides that second pair part. Immediately following this adjacency pair is a greeting-greeting adjacency pair (lines 5-6). And we can imagine there might be additional pairs following these, such as "how's it going," "fine." [2] So one simple structure that we might find in a segment of talk is a series of adjacency pairs, either different kinds of pairs as in the phone call above, or a series of the same kind of pairs as in Data Segment 3.3.

(3.3) [ID v. HT, 6, 1638]
10 Q: What is your occupation
11 A: I am a case worker for the Department of
12   Health and Welfare
13 Q: How long have you been employed in the same
14   capacity that you do have now
15 A: Three years and some months, close to
16   three and a half
17 Q: What is the general nature and scope of . . .

Here we see a series of question-answer adjacency pairs. During the taking of testimony in the courtroom, such a series can continue for a very long time. This lengthy, repetitive structure is not common in casual conversation (although shorter series of question-answer adjacency pairs are). That may be one thing that leads us to recognize such a segment as *not* part of a conversation.

Heritage (1984b) reminds us that adjacency pairs work the way they do because participants orient toward making them work, much as if trying to obey a regulative rule governing adjacency pairs. This normative orientation is visible not only in the routine occurrence of completed adjacency pairs, but also when participants think that adjacency pair norms have not been properly followed, as in Data Segments 3.4 and 3.5.

(3.4) [Nofsinger, 1973]
1 C: Anne
2 A: ((silence))
3 C: Anne
4 A: What

(3.5) [Nofsinger, 1973]
((Jim turns from another conversation))
1 J: Did somebody over there say "Jim"?
2 U: No
3 J: Oh ((turns back to the other conversation))

In both of these segments, a participant orients to the incompleteness (or possible incompleteness) of an adjacency pair that Schegloff (1972) calls a "summons-answer pair." In such a pair, one participant produces a summons (a sort of request that another person confirm his or her communicative availability) and the person summoned produces an answer that displays whether he or she is ready to converse. In the "Anne" segment (3.4), C directs a summons at A, but A fails to answer. We can see that a second pair part is expected here because C "goes looking" for the missing answer by repeating the summons. In the "Jim" segment (3.5), J checks to see whether someone had summoned him. This reveals J's concern that one ought to answer a proper summons. This and other evidence indicates that the adjacency pair is a normative structure in which participants orient to the rule that when a speaker produces a first pair part, "a second speaker should relevantly produce a second pair part . . . immediately on completion of the first" (Heritage, 1984b, p. 247).

We have seen so far that adjacency pairs are pairs of conversational actions by different speakers, in which the first action creates an opening or expectation in the conversation for a second action. We have also seen that conversational segments can be constructed by stringing together several adjacency pairs. But there are more complicated structures in which an adjacency pair may have a special relationship to other such pairs in the segment. For example, the summons-answer pair discussed above is not "just another" adjacency pair, but rather one that foreshadows or projects subsequent talk (possibly, subsequent adjacency pairs). We now examine various ways in which one adjacency pair can relate to another besides merely being in the same segment of talk.

❑ Adjacency Pair Sequences

Imagine that you are about to invite someone to go to the movies or attend a party with you, but you are uncertain whether he or she might have a conflict. Or imagine that you have been invited somewhere but are not sure about exactly what sort of occasion it is and whether you want to attend. These types of situations require that participants do some checking before they produce a first pair part (an invitation) or respond with a second pair part (an acceptance or refusal). Participants who check things out can often avoid producing actions that are offensive, doomed to failure, or otherwise ill advised. The action (or tactic) of checking before you "leap" often results in structures where one adjacency pair is linked to another in a closely integrated way. Let us look first at the matter of preparing for an upcoming action.

PRESEQUENCES

A common tactic in conversation is to check out the situation before performing some action. Participants routinely inquire about the status of other participants, or the status of certain elements of the situation prior to making a request, invitation, or other action that attempts to engage someone's cooperation. Such preliminary inquiries may even precede the telling of stories or the announcement of news (Levinson, 1983, pp. 349-352). Where such a preliminary action is itself the first part of an adjacency pair and is followed by a second

pair part, we call the resulting structure a *presequence*. Consider
Data Segment 3.6.

(3.6) [field notes]
1 B: Uh, are you gonna have access to the car about
2   five thirty or six today
3 E: Uh:: yeah I think so. Why?
4 B: Cause I'm gonna need a ride down to . . .

The adjacency pair formed by B's question in lines 1-2 and E's
answer in line 3 is a presequence. Notice that it seems to lead
up to a request for a ride (B's utterance in line 4) and actually
projects that such a request may be forthcoming. Participants
can predict from such a sequence what type of action is likely
to come next. In this case, we have a question-answer pair—the
presequence—that prepares for a request-agreement (or re-
quest-rejection) pair. Typically, presequences establish information relevant to how workable the projected action will be. "Are
you busy Saturday night" checks out the recipient's willingness
and availability for participation in some Saturday-evening
activity. In the "need a ride" segment (3.6), participants know
that a primary reason for E to reject B's request for a ride would
be that E does not have a car. In such a circumstance, a request
for a ride is sure to fail. So *before* making the request for a ride,
B checks out that condition by asking for the pertinent information. In this book, when we refer only to the first pair part of a
presequence (B's question, in this case), we will use the term
pre, or use that term as a prefix combined with the name of the
projected action—prerequest, in this case. In this book, the term
presequence will be reserved for the complete adjacency pair.
(For a discussion of a variety of uses of the pre, see Beach &
Dunning, 1982.)

   Another common presequence is the preannouncement followed by a go-ahead (or perhaps by a delay or rejection of the
impending announcement). This often precedes the telling of
news (as in, "Did you hear what happened to Mark?") and
serves to double check whether other participants have already

heard about it—in which case it is not really news and should be designed differently. In Data Segment 3.7, the participants are constructing a true/false exam, reading draft questions to each other. So the "announcement" that is projected by the presequence is the reading of one person's questions.

(3.7) [Aakhus, 1988, p. 138]
68 W: True false are not har:d (0.4) to wri:te
69   (0.5)
70 T: No (0.7) I got a couple=
71 W: =Okay=
72 T: =(   ) an aggressive attitude reflects . . .

T's "I got a couple" projects the reading of his question and gets him a quick go-ahead in line 71 (note the equal signs indicating that "Okay" follows immediately after "couple" and that T's next utterance is latched onto the end of "Okay"). This presequence, in effect, reserves the next turn for T and may function to give him an additional turn later to present his other question. We will take up issues related to conversational turn taking in Chapter 4.

We said above that participants can predict from a presequence what kind of action is likely to follow, but it is more correct to say that they can predict from the pre (for example, a prerequest or preannouncement). That is, recipients can project from the first pair part alone what sort of action might follow the presequence. An utterance such as "What are you doing Saturday night" can easily be interpreted by competent participants as a preinvitation or prerequest, and "Guess what happened at the office" can be seen as a preannouncement. This being the case, it is possible for the recipient of the pre to influence the outcome of the conversation by his or her selection of a second pair part. As we saw in the "need a ride" segment (3.6), E affirms that he has access to a car at the relevant time. With this important condition fulfilled, B proceeds with the request for a ride. But suppose E had responded to B's prerequest by denying that a car would be available; B would likely not have made the request for a ride. In such a case, the outcome of the presequence results in the projected action either not occurring at all or being modified to fit the circumstances revealed in the presequence. A response of "Oh, I'm busy Saturday night" may avoid the projected invitation and the need to reject it. Data Segment 3.8 dramatically illustrates the projection of an action even when the presequence develops in a way that suspends that action.

(3.8) [Levinson, 1983, p. 358]
1 A: Hullo I was wondering whether you were intending to
2   go to Popper's talk this afternoon
3 B: Not today I'm afraid I can't really make it to this one
4 A: Ah okay
5 B: You wanted me to record it didn't you heh!
6 A: Yeah heheh

This pre (A's lines 1-2) projects a request of some sort as the relevant next action. But B's answer (line 3) reveals that the necessary conditions for the request to be successful are not present—so A does not produce the request, but merely acknowledges B's answer. In line 5, B identifies the projected action (namely, that A was going to request that B record Popper's talk), even though it did not occur. This identification is correct, as judged by A's line 6. Because of this projection of a future action, we can regard an adjacency pair such as lines 1-3 as a *pre*sequence even when the projected action does not occur. The presequence, then, is an adjacency pair that precedes and projects some other conversational action (often another adjacency pair). As we have seen, a more or less specific type of action can be projected. Some presequences, however, project only continued conversation. In our discussion of the summons-answer adjacency pair (the "Anne" segment, 3.4), we noted that further talk is projected. But the projected talk need not be any particular future action. A summons-answer is a nonspecific presequence, as illustrated in Data Segment 3.9.

(3.9) [Nofsinger, 1973]
1 A: Hey, listen
2 B: What
3 A: Why don't we go over to . . .

In this case, the presequence (lines 1-2) leads to a suggestion or invitation in line 3. Notice, however, that it could just as well have resulted in a question ("How was your trip?"), a complaint ("I'm getting sick and tired of your cookie crumbs"), a congrat-ulations, a statement, and so on. Such a presequence projects *some* talk, but not any specific action.

For a final example of a presequence, let us examine again the opening of a telephone conversation (Data Segment 3.2). We did not discuss the first two lines of that segment: the ringing of the phone in line 1 and the answerer's hello in line 2. We said that lines 3-4 were an identification adjacency pair and lines 5-6 were a greeting-greeting pair. But what about H's hello in line 2—Does that belong or fit with any other action? And why does the answerer speak first in a telephone conversation, anyway? It is the caller who knows both who is calling and who the answerer is likely to be, so why doesn't the caller speak up? Schegloff (1972) suggests that the first communicative action in a telephone call is the caller *summoning* an answerer through the ringing of the phone. According to this analysis, the first adjacency pair in that conversation (Segment 3.2) is the ringing of the phone (the first pair part) and the answerer's hello (the second pair part). That is, the call begins (lines 1-2) with a summons-answer presequence that projects some continuing conversation.

When a pre allows the projection of a specific type of upcom-ing action, participants often omit one or more steps in the various sequences (see Levinson, 1983, pp. 349-356). Data Seg-ment 3.10 displays an inquiry about whether the district attor-ney (DA) has an offer to make in the plea bargaining of a disorderly conduct case. This is followed not by an answer to the inquiry, but by the offer itself and its acceptance by the public defender (PD).

(3.10) [Maynard, 1984, p. 94]
1 PD: Is there a offer in that case
2 DA: I would say in this case uh a fine, seventy five dollars
3 PD: Arright

In its most elaborate form, we might imagine line 1 as the first pair part of a *pre*sequence and line 2 as the second pair part of the *projected* sequence: "Is there a offer in that case"; "Yes"; "What is it"; "I would say in this case uh a fine." But the projectability of such related sequences allows a participant (DA, in this case) to move directly to the second action of the second adjacency pair (the offer itself). This analysis suggests an alternative way of handling the problem of indirect speech acts, discussed previously in Chapter 2 (see Levinson, 1983, pp. 356-364). We said that utterances that make reference to a participant's ability, interest, or willingness to perform some future behavior are often interpreted as a *request* for that behavior. Similarly, an utterance that mentions the speaker's desire that a participant do something is an indirect way of requesting the person to do it. For example, "Can you reach that back-pack?" and "I'd like another helping of casserole" are requests (for the backpack and for more casserole). We would not normally treat these utterances as being merely a yes/no question and a statement about the speaker's likes. In some cases, an indirect speech act can be regarded as a pre that is treated by participants as one of the actions that was projected to occur later in the sequence. In the plea bargaining segment (3.10), an utterance (line 1) that projects the impending *solicitation* of an offer (that projects a "What is it?" from PD) is treated as being that solicitation. That is, it results not merely in an answer as to whether there is an offer, but in the offer itself. The importance of this for understanding the conduct of conversation is that actual sequence patterns may be incomplete (missing a first or second pair part), yet participants will have no trouble interpreting each other's talk. Adjacency pairs organize conversational action in such a way that participants can project what a set of complete sequences might be like and skip right to the heart of the matter: "Have you seen that new movie over at the shopping center?" "I'd love to!"

We have seen that one way in which two adjacency pairs can be relevant to each other (besides merely occurring together) is that one—the presequence—can involve the projection or setting up of a subsequent one. There is another arrangement of adjacency pairs in which one actually occurs inside the other, as we shall now see.

INSERTION SEQUENCES

Another tactic for checking out what a participant means is to request clarification immediately *after* the speaker's first pair part, but *before* producing a second pair part in reply. Any recipient of a first pair part may experience a variety of difficulties in knowing how to respond. One potential problem is that a speaker's propositional meaning may not be clear: "Would you like some dessert?" is probably an offer (as discussed above in connection with presequences), but what is meant by "dessert"? Or a speaker's actional (illocutionary) meaning may not be clear: "At this point in the evening we usually have some apple pie" could be either an offer or the beginning of an explanation of why there won't be any apple pie tonight. Another problem, related to our discussion of presequences, is that what the action is leading up to may not be entirely clear. Recipients can cope with such problems by inserting a clarifying question (or other relevant action) just after the first pair part. This clarifying question is itself the first part of an adjacency pair and the answer to it is the second part. We call such an adjacency pair occurring within another pair an *insertion sequence*.

In Data Segment 3.11, S has been trying to get through to G on the phone, and finally does.

(3.11) [Jefferson, 1986, p. 168, simplified]
1 S: Who w'yih ta:lking to.
2   (0.6)

```
3  G:  Jis no:w?
4  S:  .hhhh No I called be-like between
5      ele ven
                [
6  G:       I: wasn't talkeen tuh a:nybuddy. . . .
```

It seems that S's utterance in line 1 is a question and it does, in fact, eventually get an answer. But neither the half-second silence in line 2 nor G's utterance in line 3 can count as that answer. In this instance, the answer occurs (in line 6) after G and S have each produced an intervening utterance. Yet lines 1 and 6 still seem to be a proper adjacency pair and participants do orient to the occurrence of the second pair part in cases like this. If G were to fail to produce an answer after line 5, S might well ask the question again. The reason this adjacency pair is not disrupted by the intervening talk is that what intervenes is another adjacency pair—an insertion sequence—designed to clarify S's original question. In discussing the characteristics of adjacency pairs, we said that the two actions are adjacent to each other. For example, an answer directly follows a question, an acceptance (or a rejection) directly follows an invitation, and so on. Close examination of everyday talk, however, reveals that this is not always true. First and second parts of adjacency pairs are frequently separated by other talk designed to clarify what the first pair part is getting at (as in the phone conversation between S and G above).

So an adjacency pair can operate across intervening utterances of this type. When the insertion sequence is completed, the second pair part of the original adjacency pair again becomes relevant. Data Segment 3.12 presents a more complicated structure involving insertion sequences.

(3.12) [Schegloff, 1980, p. 137, abbreviated]
```
1  P:  How are yuh.
2  H:  Pretty goo:d.
3  P:  Yih gon'be down inna morning?
4  H:  Well sir now I' gon'tell yih sum'n.
5      I'm runnin a g'rage sale here .hh
6  P:  Yer havin a g'rage sale,
```

7 H: Yeah .hh
8 P: Well fer cryin out loud.
9 H: If I c'n possibly get away I'll be do:wn.

In line 3, P reminds H of a project and solicits a commitment from H to participate. The commitment, conditional though it is, appears in line 9 and completes an adjacency pair. But H's first response to P's reminder presents some preliminary information (lines 4-5), a sort of objection or reservation, which can be seen as the reason the commitment will be only partial. P's expression of surprise in line 8 ("Well fer cryin out loud") also occurs between the first and second parts of the solicit-commitment adjacency pair. It acknowledges H's reservation. This reservation-acknowledgment pair (lines 4-5 and 8) is an insertion sequence that modifies what sort of commitment can be expected from H. Yet another insertion sequence (lines 6 and 7) comes between H's preliminary information (the reservation) and P's expression of surprise. It serves to confirm the facts of H's reservation: Its first pair part is a confirmation request and its second is the confirmation ("Yeah"). So in this example, we can see one insertion sequence *nested* within another.

Insertion sequences, then, can essentially occur within any other adjacency pair, including presequences and other insertion sequences. A *series* of insertion sequences can also occur, as in Data Segment 3.13 (a call to the police).

(3.13) [Whalen & Zimmerman, 1987, p. 174]
 1 D: Mid-City Emergency
 2 C: Um yeah (.) somebody jus' vandalized my car,
 3 D: What's your address.
 4 C: Thirty three twenty two: Elm.
 5 D: Is this uh house or an apartment.
 6 C: Ih tst uh house
 7 D: Uh- your las' name.
 8 C: Minsky,
 9 D: How you spell it.
10 C: M. I. N. S. K. Y.
11 D: Wull sen' somebody out to see you.

With line 2, the caller gets to the reason for the call and gets down to business. We recognize that C's action in line 2 is more than a mere report. It is an attempt to get the police to respond by sending an officer to C's location, starting an investigation, and so forth. The reply that promises those sorts of things occurs in line 11. Yet in between these two pair parts there are four question-answer insertion sequences: lines 3-4, 5-6, 7-8, and 9-10! Each of them more or less meets the requirement that insertion sequences be relevant to clarifying or modifying the sequence (adjacency pair) that they are inserted in. In this case, getting the caller's name and exact location can be seen as relevant not only to actually sending out an officer, but also to the record keeping that is necessary in organizations of this kind. And we can see that even a series of several insertion sequences does not disrupt the connection between a first and second pair part.

So the actions in lines 2 and 11 form a complaint and promise-of-action adjacency pair that maintains its structural integrity across eight intervening speaker turns. This suggests that our description of adjacency pairs as having two *adjacent* actions should be modified. Schegloff (1972) uses the term *conditional relevance* to name the connection between the two parts of an adjacency pair (pp. 363-370). Given the occurrence of a first pair part (that is, conditional on a first pair part), a second pair part is relevant in the next turn and participants expect it there. The actual occurrence of the second pair part can be postponed by one or more insertion sequences, but it becomes relevant again in the following turn. Thus it is the *expectation* of the second pair part—conditional relevance—rather than actual adjacency that binds the adjacency pair together. Jacobs and Jackson (1983a) would argue that this is due to participants' understanding of the functions of conversational actions in any particular language game. For example, participants in the telephone call to the police (Segment 3.13) know that the point of reporting a crime is to get a commitment of help from the police (and, eventually, the help itself). They know that the caller's report or complaint should eventually elicit a promise of help—even after considerable intervening talk—and that the insertion sequences do not fulfill this functional requirement. So they continue to orient toward the relevance of the second pair part until it either occurs or remedial action is undertaken to cope with its absence.

In summary, many (but not all) conversational actions are organized into sequences called adjacency pairs. The first action of the pair (the first pair part) opens a "slot" in the conversation for the second pair part, making the occurrence of that second action conditionally relevant (expected). Participants use various combinations of adjacency pairs to conduct conversation and everyday business. In particular, presequences are used to prepare for and lead up to some conversational action by checking out the conditions necessary for that action's success. And insertion sequences are used to clarify a first pair part before replying to it (a second pair part). Conversational structures of various complexity result from participants' moment-by-moment use of adjacency pairs. At this point, we should note that even though adjacent placement is not the glue that binds adjacency pairs together, it is still one of the most important relationships between utterances in conversation. As mentioned in Chapter 2, it is in the very next turn that a participant normally displays his or her interpretation of the previous speaker's turn (Heritage, 1984b, p. 245). Let us now examine this and other relationships among conversational actions.

❏ Other Action Relationships

Conditional relevance, the relationship between the first and second parts of an adjacency pair, is a very strong connection between two conversational actions, but it is by no means the only important one or even the most common. Participants give a special interpretation to two utterances when they occur immediately adjacent to each other. And any utterance can influence a subsequent one, whether or not they form an

adjacency pair. We now examine some of the relationships—
other than conditional relevance—that hold between conversational actions.

When your conversational partner replies to your invitation
to play tennis by saying, "I'd love to!" and you then ask, "What
time?" we expect that you will be interpreted as asking what
time would be convenient for tennis. We would be surprised
and disconcerted if you were interpreted as asking what time it
is now or what time would be good for grocery shopping.
"What time?" will be given a certain interpretation because of
the previous utterance that is adjacent to it. Participants routinely depend on the immediately prior utterance to help each
other make sense of the current one, even if the two actions are
not an adjacency pair. At the same time, the current utterance
is an indication of how its speaker interpreted the prior one. In
our hypothetical example, "What time?" can be seen as asking
about specific arrangements for playing tennis partly because
the prior utterance ("I'd love to!") was interpreted as accepting
an invitation to play tennis. And "What time?" shows that its
speaker is treating the prior utterance as an acceptance.

This ongoing judgment of each utterance against those immediately adjacent to it provides participants with a continually updated (and, if need be, corrected) understanding of
the conversation. It is a routine source of *intersubjective understanding* among people who interact in everyday life (Heritage,
1984b, pp. 254-260). That is, each person constructs his or her
own subjective meanings for talk (and other events)—subjective in the sense that each person's brain does this work. But
social interaction proceeds smoothly in part because the meanings that each person's brain creates are similar to the meanings
constructed by other people's brains (similar enough, that is,
for practical purposes). Thus we say that social interactants
have *inter*subjective understandings about many everyday
things. The way participants treat adjacent utterances is a major

contributor to this. We can track this process as it operates in Data Segment 3.14.

(3.14) [Button & Casey, 1985, p. 43 (from Goodwin), simplified]
1 A: How's Tina doin.
2 J: Oh she's doin goo:d.
3 A: Is she I heard she got divo:rc:ed.=
4 J: =Mm hmm?
5 A: (.) Is she?
6 J: (sh)sposeuh get rema:rried again thou:gh,
7   next couple A'weeks,=
8 A: =Oh yer kiddee:n. Who's she marryin.

In line 1, A asks a rather general question about Tina. This action (which Button & Casey, 1985, term an "itemized news inquiry") is commonly used to bring up some topic for discussion without offering or demanding any particular piece of information.

We can see that J (in line 2) treats the question as very general indeed, perhaps even as requiring only a ritual (not necessarily truthful or informative) response. Thus line 2 displays a certain understanding by J of line 1. But in the very next utterance, we can see that A does not accept such an understanding of "How's Tina doin." The statement that A presents (in 3) for confirmation or disconfirmation shows that the topic A is really trying to open up is Tina's divorce. So line 3 is designed to correct J's apparent understanding of A's first utterance: It is an attempt to get J to talk about a major newsworthy item related to Tina. Note that while lines 1 and 2 are first and second parts of an adjacency pair, lines 2 and 3 do not have that same relationship. J's utterance does not require any particular reply or set of replies from A. For example, in addition to A's actual utterance, line 3 could also have legitimately been a mere acknowledgment ("Glad to hear it"), a similar inquiry about someone else ("And how 'bout Fred"), a newsworthy item about someone else ("Did I tell you Betsy crashed her bike"), and so forth. The point is that we hear line 3 as a correction of what line 2 seems to display because the two actions are *adjacent* to each other, not because they are parts of the same adjacency pair.

Now examine J's reply in line 4. "Mm hmm" is an answer to line 3, but it treats that utterance as nothing but a confirmation request, rather than as a prompt for a more informative answer. We can see that A's next utterance treats line 4 as inadequate; A seems to be prompting J for an elaboration and, as it turns out, gets one in lines 6-7. As in the earlier portion of the data segment, each next adjacent utterance updates our understanding of what was being done in earlier utterances, of how the participants interpreted each other, and of whether an interpretation was accepted or corrected in the following utterance. This updated intersubjective understanding of the ongoing conversation is produced by the participants *for each other* and provides the basis for their continuing talk. It is secondarily available to us as observers. So the adjacent positioning of two conversational actions (not parts of the same adjacency pair) is a major resource that participants use to indicate to each other how their utterances are to be understood. We will see more about how this process works in Chapter 5.

OCCASIONING

Virtually any utterance has the potential to be taken up as the focus of the conversation or to trigger an utterance by someone else that becomes the focus. Participants are skilled in using utterances as a resource for constructing another utterance. We will say that one utterance *occasions* a later one, or that certain talk was *occasioned by* certain earlier talk.[3] Jefferson (1978), for example, describes how stories are occasioned by utterances in the local conversation in which they occur. Data Segment 3.15 is an instance of this.

(3.15) [Jefferson, 1978, p. 224, modified]
1 K: He was terrific the whole time we were there.
2 L: I know what you mean. Wh'n they- my sister and
3   her boyfriend ((story continues))

Something in what K has said (perhaps specifically what he says in line 1) triggers a story for L. She then displays that there is going to be a connection ("I know what you mean") and begins to introduce the story. Both K's talk and the first sentence of L's *occasion* the story. Such occasioning relationships can operate over a distance of several speaking turns, as Mandelbaum's (1987) work shows. She analyzes stories in which early remarks by one potential teller of a story are commented on by another potential teller and then brought up again by the first. In Mandelbaum's terminology, a remote approach to a story is first forwarded, then ratified as the story begins (pp. 149-155). This process involves several utterances by several speakers, but there is a sense in which the story is occasioned by the very early utterance of the first teller. Common examples of occasioning would include the mention of a location (e.g., "Los Angeles") occasioning a comment or question about someone who lives there, or the mention of a family member occasioning an utterance about another member of the family. Thus K's and B's utterances (lines 39 and 42) occasion K's question about B's dad (line 45) in Data Segment 3.16.

(3.16) [Craig & Tracy, 1983a, B-K, pp. 305-306]
39 K: Oh where's your mom living.
          ((two utterances omitted))
42 B: My mother lives in Minneapolis.
43 K: Hmm::!
44 B: Which is easy and I visit her on vacations a lot.
45 K: Um hmm? And your dad lives in Philadelphia . . .

It seems that there are many ways in which occasioning works. As research on conversational processes continues, the concept of one utterance occasioning or triggering another may be expanded, or may be subdivided into several different relationships.

UTTERANCES IN A SERIES

One other sequential structure is worth our attention at this point. Individual utterances or adjacency pairs are sometimes strung together in a *series* of very similar items. For example, white-water rafting enthusiasts might produce a series of "checklist" pairs: "Raft" "Check" "Paddles" "Check" "Life jackets" "Oops!" Any two participants may alternate questions and answers in such a way that a string of Q-A pairs is produced in which all the pairs have equal status (for example, none of them is a presequence or insertion sequence). Or one participant may produce statements or instructions in alternation with another participant's acknowledgments (sometimes called *receipt tokens*), as in Data Segment 3.17.

(3.17) [Psathas, 1986, p. 245]
 5 A: Get on the free:way,
 6 C: mm hmm,
 7 A: an' get off at Burbank Boulevard.
 8 C: mm hmm,
 9 A: head toward the mountains,
10 C: mm hmm,

In this giving and receiving of directions, the items that compose the series are direction-and-receipt pairs. This turns out to be one type of list. Another activity in which a series structure arises is when participants are *explicitly* generating a list and they design each of their utterances to be an item in that list (things to do tonight, for example, or people to invite to a party). In this case, we might have a series of individual actions (suggestions, for example) rather than a series of action pairs.

The concept of preference is not based on participants' psychological desires or motivations.

PREFERENCE

Of all the technical concepts associated with conversation-analytic approaches to everyday talk, none has more potential for misleading or confusing the student of conversation than that of *preference*.[4] We must begin with the reminder that, while a first pair part makes conditionally relevant a second pair part, more than one specific type of second action can usually "fill the slot." Invitations, for example, can properly be either accepted or rejected (declined). Requests can properly be either granted or refused, bets can be accepted or not, and so on. In these cases, either choice of second pair part will be regarded as fulfilling the requirement established by the first pair part. But these alternatives are frequently not treated by participants as equivalent choices. Accepting and rejecting an invitation do not have the same value for participants. Schegloff (1988) says that such alternatives are not "equivalent" (p. 456). Responses to first parts of adjacency pairs and, as we shall see, responses to certain other "first" actions are organized by a preference system in which some second actions are treated (by participants) as *preferred* and others as *dispreferred* (see Heritage, 1984b, pp. 265-269). Now for the tricky part: Despite the use of these two terms, the concept of preference is *not* based on participants' psychological desires or motivations. The preference system uses various degrees of structural complexity to enhance the performance of preferred responses, inhibit the performance of dispreferred responses, and mark the dispreferred ones so that their status is displayed. Preferred second pair parts tend to be structurally simple, allowing quicker and easier production; dispreferred second pair parts tend to be structurally complex. Compare the responses to the two invitations in Data Segments 3.18 and 3.19.

(3.18) [Atkinson & Drew, 1979, p. 58]
1 B: Why don't you come up and <u>see</u> me some times
2 A: ⌈I would like to

(3.19) [Atkinson & Drew, 1979, p. 58]
1 B: Uh if you'd care to come over and visit a little while
2   this morning I'll give you a cup of <u>co</u>ffee.
3 A: hehh Well that's awfully sweet of you,
4   I don't think I can make it this morning
5   .hh uhm I'm running an ad in the paper and- and uh
6   I have to stay near the phone.

In the first segment (3.18), A's acceptance of B's invitation is very quick and fairly direct. In fact, A begins accepting before B's utterance is finished (note how line 2 overlaps the end of line 1). Acceptance of an invitation is a preferred reply and is easily produced before anything can interfere with it. Notice how this contrasts with the complexity of A's rejection of B's invitation in the next data segment (3.19). As Atkinson and Drew (1979, pp. 58-59) remark, the actual rejection (line 4) is delayed in its production first by a little laugh or breath ("hehh"), then by "well," and then by a statement of appreciation. Furthermore, the rejection itself is designed to be somewhat tentative or reluctant ("I don't think") and limited in scope ("this morning"). Finally, the rejection is accompanied by an explanation—an *account* (lines 5-6).[5] These components of A's rejection are typical of a dispreferred second pair part. Together with other common components, such as a short silence before replying, they mark certain alternative responses as dispreferred and increase the likelihood that they will be

avoided. Note, for example, that B could have jumped back
into the conversation just after "well" and modified the invitation to the next day or next week. That might have resulted in
an acceptance. We will examine this process more carefully in
Chapter 5. And we must once again remind ourselves that the
dispreferred status of A's rejection does not depend on A's
psychological state. The way the rejection in lines 3-6 is designed constitutes a public display of the dispreferred status
of rejections, rather than proof that A wants to "come over and
visit." Such a display is quite compatible with A wanting to
stay home and being very pleased not to have to visit B that
morning.

So many of the actions we have discussed as being first parts
of adjacency pairs make relevant several possible second actions, one of which (typically) will be a preferred second pair
part and the others dispreferred. Which type of second action

has preferred status may be inherently related to the type of first action. For example, the point or function of an invitation is first of all to get an acceptance, and it might be said that many other first actions are "built" to get a particular type of second action in reply. Schegloff (1988) refers to this type of preference, "related to the business" that an adjacency pair is designed to do, as "structure-based preference" (p. 453). Another line of research on preference focuses on instances where we know which second action is preferred and which is dispreferred *because* of the different structural complexities in the utterances. For example, it does not seem at first that statements of evaluation, *assessments*, as they are called, are inherently built to get agreement. The utterance "That's a really exciting book" certainly occasions agreement or disagreement in the next utterance, but it is not at all clear that its function is to get agreement in the way that the function of a request is to get a grant. Yet we know that replies to assessments (with one notable exception) overwhelmingly exhibit agreements that are designed as preferred and disagreements designed as dispreferred. Schegloff (1988) calls this type of preference "practice-based preference" (p. 453).

Pomerantz (1978, 1984, 1989), a leading investigator of these "second assessments," finds that agreements with a prior assessment are produced quickly and simply, as in Data Segment 3.20.

(3.20) [Pomerantz, 1984, p. 62]
((B refers to a bridge party which both attended))
1 B: Well, it was fun Cla ire,
2 A: Yeah, I enjoyed every minute of it.

Note the design of a preferred reply: A's second assessment is an agreement token ("Yeah") positioned early in the utterance, which actually overlaps B. Disagreements, on the other hand, tend to be delayed and accompanied by components that modify or soften the disagreement. See Sacks (1987) for a recently published version of some of his early work on preference. The exception (mentioned above) to this systematic preference for agreement is that when the first assessment is a self-deprecation (the speaker is critical of him- or herself), the preferred second assessment is a *dis*agreement. Agreements to self-deprecations have the dispreferred design, as in Data Segment 3.21, where L's agreement with W's self-characterization as Pavlov's dog is first delayed two seconds and then done only tentatively ("I suppose").

(3.21) [Pomerantz, 1984, pp. 90-91]
1 W: . . . Do you know what I was all that time?
2 L: (No).
3 W: Pavlov's dog.
4   (2.0)
5 L: (I suppose),

Preference, then, is a system that organizes certain types of second actions in a way that gives a kind of priority to one particular choice from a set of alternatives and relegates other choices to being delayed, structurally complex, and appearing "reluctant" (Bilmes, 1988, p. 173). In Chapter 5, we will examine in more detail the impact of the preference system on participants' understanding of each other.

❏ Summary

Conversational actions are frequently provided for or occasioned by earlier actions. Participants use this earlier talk to help them interpret the current utterance; they especially use the adjacent (immediately prior) talk to make sense of what is being said at the moment. One particularly powerful kind of occasioning is found in adjacency pairs (such as question-answer, invitation-acceptance, or request-refusal), in which the first of a pair of actions makes relevant a limited and specific set of second actions by the other speaker. This second pair part can be separated from its first pair part (that is, delayed) by the insertion of another adjacency pair—an insertion sequence (often a question-answer or confirmation request-answer pair). But there is a continuing orientation to the expected occurrence of the second pair part of the original adjacency pair, despite the insertion of these other utterances. This connection between the first and second parts of an adjacency pair is called conditional relevance. Adjacency pairs are also used to precede and prepare for conversational actions. In this role they are called presequences. Additional, more complex structures of talk can also be constructed with various combinations of adjacency pairs and other action groupings.

> *The type of action an utterance turns out to be depends crucially on its place in some conversational structure.*

We have seen that conversational action—which is, in effect, social action—is organized into various structures by those who produce it. Indeed, what type of action an utterance turns out to be depends crucially on its place in some conversational structure. One of the major weaknesses of speech act theory as described in Chapter 2 is that it does not seriously take this fact into account. Some action structures (particularly adjacency pairs) have a compelling quality about them because participants orient to their proper completion. We have seen that participants will "go looking for" missing second pair parts, or attempt to account for their absence. This may be due to participants' overall understanding of the collection of language "games" that we call conversation. Participants recognize that the function of first pair parts cannot be achieved without the matching second pair parts (see Jacobs & Jackson, 1983a). At least one type of preference operating on the production of second pair parts suggests that participants employ such a strategic command of language: Where a first part has as its immediate point the elicitation of a specific type of second part, that type of second is the preferred reply. But whatever the reason, it is empirically clear that participants do orient toward the adjacency pair as a normative or enforceable system. Other structures (utterances in a series, for example) are more optional, in the sense that participants do not have to account for failing to supply the next piece.

Not only is social action organized in various ways, but the actual talk that produces it is structurally organized as well. Conversational utterances occur when speakers take alternating turns at talk. Since the interpretation that is made of one's utterances depends on their sequential location in the ongoing conversation, the system by which participants acquire speaking turns in order to produce those utterances is of enormous consequence to the conduct of conversation. We examine the conversational turn-taking system next, in Chapter 4.

❏ Notes

1. It will turn out that adjacent placement, though important in its own right, is not a defining characteristic of adjacency pairs. In its place, we will use the concept of *conditional relevance* (see, for example, Levinson, 1983, pp. 304-307). I only recently discovered the term *type-connected* in the work of Harvey Sacks (1987, p. 55); other authors use the term *typed*.

2. Notice that the stress on the second "Hi" (line 6 in Data Segment 3.2) may indicate recognition of R by H, as well as greeting. For a thorough examination of the various functions of telephone openings, see Schegloff (1972, 1979).

3. Jefferson (1978) uses "sequentially implicates" rather than *occasions* (p. 245, n. 4). That is, a prior utterance sequentially implicates a later one and the later one is occasioned by it. In this book we will use *occasions* and *is occasioned by*.

4. In fact, some analysts argue that the concept of preference has confused even some seasoned veterans. Bilmes (1988) presents a somewhat different concept of preference than that used here. He argues that the original use of the term relates to the inferences that participants make on those occasions when the preferred reply is given, the dispreferred reply is given, or neither reply is given (pp. 162-166). In his view, the defining characteristic of a preferred reply is that in its absence participants infer that the dispreferred choice is intended (even if neither was actually given). He then traces developments in the literature on preference, indicating that some analysts have incorporated a psychological notion of preference.

5. See Heritage (1988) for the analysis of this use of accounts.

4

Turn Organization

Remember those times in conversation when you desperately needed to be the very next person to speak? And we have all noticed the frustration of the person who is not able to "get a word in edgewise." Up to this point, we have taken for granted the way conversational participants take turns exchanging talk. In Chapter 2, we just assumed that someone was the speaker and that he or she had one or more recipients for whom an utterance was designed. But in Chapter 3, things began to get complicated because we were considering sequences of conversational actions produced by *different* speakers. We postponed consideration of how various participants become speakers: how one "gets the floor" as speaker to produce the first pair part of an adjacency pair, or the required second part, or to make some other contribution. We have learned enough about the conduct of conversation at this point to figure out that some system for organizing utterances into turns is of vital importance to its participants. The organization of social or communicative actions into pairs, or sequences, or whatever, depends on some way of changing or alternating speakers. For example, the adjacency pair depends on two speakers coordinating the production of at least one utterance apiece. Presequences and insertion sequences further extend the number of times participants must exchange talk. And remember that positioning an utterance adjacent to another just-completed one can be very important, since that new utterance is normally interpreted as responding to the adjacently prior one and serves to display its speaker's interpretation of that prior utterance. This means that getting a turn "right now"—when one needs it—can be a serious issue. In conversation, these matters are dealt with by organizing participants' utterances into sequential *turns*.

> *Getting a turn "right now" can be a serious issue.*

Everyday life is filled with mechanisms for organizing people's activities. This frequently involves sequential or alternating turns. Guitar students at a recital perform in a sequence determined ahead of time and often published in a program. Sports fans (or concert or theater devotees) purchase tickets in a sequence determined by the individual's position in line. This is more or less determined by order of arrival (as is the "take a number" system prevalent in crowded retail and service outlets). Getting one's turn can be so important that people sometimes arrive hours or even days ahead of time to ensure an early place in line. In some cases, the order of turns is determined by the status of the participants. People who are richer, more famous, or more powerful may be served first. Each of these situations involves a system that generates single turns (one person at a time at the ticket window, for example). Some turn-organizing systems, however, operate to allow (or require) all participants to take their turns at the same time, as happens when all guests at a dinner party begin to eat when the host does. Single sequential turns are important in conversation because human beings' capacity to monitor several different spoken messages at once is limited and because some messages are responses to others and must occur later. But the organization of turns in a conversation is not determined ahead of time, nor is it fundamentally determined by wealth or fame (although these factors may influence turn taking), nor is it determined by order of arrival, in the broad sense—we do not take numbers or stand in line to talk.

❑ The Turn-Taking System

Sacks, Schegloff, and Jefferson (1978) have proposed a model of how conversational turn taking is organized that focuses on two questions: Out of what message units are turns constructed? By what practices (methods, techniques) are turns allocated to one participant or another? Let us now examine the details of turn taking in the conduct of conversation.

TURN CONSTRUCTION

Sacks et al. (1978) claim that turns are constructed out of any of four different-sized units of talk. Some turns are one word long, constructed with a single lexical item ("yes," "Mary," "twelve"). Other turns are constructed with a phrase: several words that do not constitute a sentence, that do not have both a subject and a predicate ("in the garage," "gone home," "the boss"). Others are constructed with a clause, which we might describe as a group of words that do have all the necessary components to be a sentence (both a subject and predicate), but do not constitute a stand-alone sentence because they are designed to be part of some other sentence ("the woman who gave today's lecture," "when we finish studying"). Still other turns are constructed with a full sentence ("We'll turn on the TV when we finish studying," "Kitty is going to Japan"). The important thing about each of these turn construction units is that participants can *project* where they will end—and thus where a particular turn might possibly be complete. This spot that participants recognize as the potential end of a turn, this place where a transition from one speaker to another becomes relevant, is called a "transition relevance place" by Sacks et al. (1978).[1] We will refer to this throughout the book as a *TRP*. Thus a word being used as a complete turn will have TRP at its end. So will a phrase designed to be a complete turn, as will a clause and a sentence. In conversational turn taking, the various practices that participants use to change from one speaker to another (or to give another turn to the same speaker) operate at the TRP. This makes the TRP a very important concept in our understanding the conduct of conversation.

Data Segment 4.1 exhibits several different types of turn construction units.

(4.1) [Sacks et al., 1978, p. 51]
1 A: Was last night the first time you met Missiz Kelly?
2   (1.0)
3 B: Met whom?
4 A: Missiz Kelly.
5 B: Yes.

The first turn is constructed using a sentence (line 1), the next two using phrases (lines 3-4), and the last one using a single word (line 5). In addition, we can sense that participants would probably detect a TRP (the possible completion of the turn) at the end of lines 1, 3, 4, and 5. Note that although a TRP may involve a short silence, our transcript does not mark this silence unless it is longer than "a conversational beat," as in the one-second silence in line 2. But whatever the cues that participants use to detect a TRP, whether they include a change in the pitch or volume of the voice, the end of a syntactic unit of language, a momentary silence, or some sort of body motion, it is at the TRP that transition from one speaker to another normally occurs. We now turn our attention to the way that speaking turns are *allocated* (given to, or claimed by, a conversational participant).

Sacks et al. (1978) identify three techniques by which participants determine who gets the next turn, and they propose a set of rules fixing the rights and responsibilities of the participants. Remember that speaker change should occur at a TRP. One practice for allocating the next turn is that the current speaker can choose the next speaker. This is called *current speaker selects next* (Sacks et al., 1978, p. 13). Our discussion of action sequences in Chapter 3 suggests one of the primary ways in which this can be accomplished: The current speaker directs the first pair part of an adjacency pair to some other participant. The identity of this other person can be indicated by the current speaker in various ways, including using the person's name, making eye contact, and so forth. Notice that this must be done *during* the course of the current utterance. Then, at the first TRP, the person who has been selected has exclusive rights to the next turn and is actually obligated to take that turn. Assume, for purposes of illustration, that Data Segment 4.2 occurs in a conversation of several participants.

(4.2) [Sacks et al., 1978, p. 51, simplified]
```
 1  A:  Uh you been down here before  havenche.
                                    [
 2  B:                                Yeh.
```

The current speaker, A, selects B as next speaker by directing a question to B (line 1). Note A's stress on "you," which we will assume may have been accompanied by other behaviors or context identifying B. The next turn is then taken by B (line 2), who produces an answer to the question. No other participant may take the turn following A—to do so would violate turn-taking etiquette for conversation. In effect, current speaker selects next has priority over the other methods of allocating the turn because it is employed before the TRP and because once it has been used no other participant may be selected as next speaker. This is a powerful technique not only for determining the next speaker but for extending the conversation another turn.

Before discussing the other two techniques for turn allocation, we should clear up a feature of this last segment (4.2) that seems to contradict the statement that speaker change occurs at the end of a turn construction unit (that is, at the TRP). B's "Yeh" clearly overlaps A's "havenche." Why does B's turn begin before the end of A's turn? Remember that participants are able to project the end of a turn construction unit and thus the occurrence of a TRP. In this case, A produces a sentence that projects to completion just after the word "before." Producing a statement for another participant to confirm or deny is a routine conversational action, and "Uh you been down here before" can be seen as a complete turn construction unit. B may have projected a TRP at that point and gone ahead to take a normal turn. The overlap would then be caused by A adding the tag question "havenche" to the end of a turn that B is treating as already complete. The point to be learned from this example is that the smoothness and coordination we frequently find in conversation depends on the skill levels of the participants and on their ability to respond to unexpected events.

How is the next turn allocated if the current speaker does not select the next one? Not every utterance is part of an adjacency pair, and many utterances do not require a particular participant to respond. What happens, for example, after someone makes an offhand observation or comment, or after someone answers a prior question? Sacks et al. (1978) say that if current speaker does not select next, then at the TRP any listener may begin a turn; that is, he or she may *self-select* (p. 13). Furthermore, the first listener to do so then has exclusive rights to the turn and any others who have begun to speak should stop. This rule puts a premium on starting quickly, since several participants may self-select and failure to be first may mean either that one drops out or that one continues with the risk of being judged as "butting in" on someone else's turn. Tannen (1986) suggests that serious miscoordination problems can arise when one participant is a quick self-starter and another is slower to begin a turn (perhaps because he or she needs a more clearly marked TRP). Not only do such people have difficulty conversing with one another, but they often attribute negative intentions or characteristics to each other (for example, he wants to hog the entire conversation; or, she won't talk, she must not be interested in me). Sacks et al. (1978) point out that the existence of the self-selection option means that if current speakers are to be assured of selecting the next speaker they must accomplish it before the TRP, since at the TRP any listener may get the next turn.

Data Segment 4.3 involves several instances of listeners self-selecting. Six people are having breakfast, five of them seated around a table; B and J have just talked about someone who went skiing with his dark glasses on under his (tinted) goggles. B has just self-selected and begins to talk about yesterday's skiing.

(4.3) [Cliff Story, simplified]
49 B: Just like I did yesterday
50   I might as well have had my
51   dark glasses on under my goggles.
52 W: Yeh. _[( )_]
53 B: [[]I cou-[]]
54   I couldn't see anything.
55   (2.6)
56 J: Well it's amazing tha:tuh (.) I picked
57   the right day to get sick on.

B's remark in lines 49-51 is not directed at anyone in particular, but is a statement to the entire group. Furthermore, it is not the first part of an adjacency pair (it does not require one of just a few specific second actions). So B has not used current speaker selects next. At the end of that turn, W self-selects with an acknowledgment of B's remark and a few additional words that are not clear on the tape (line 52). It does not seem that W has used current speaker selects next, so B's next utterance (line 53) is probably another self-selection. Notice that either the listener misprojects a TRP after "Yeh," or the current speaker suddenly elects to continue just after the TRP (we will consider this method of allocating turns in a moment). The resulting overlap is similar to the one in the "havenche" segment (4.2). In any case, B breaks off his utterance and restarts it again in line 54 (another self-selection). Then, after a fairly lengthy silence, J self-selects (lines 56-57). In this segment, then, who gets to speak is determined by who self-selects, when and how quickly they do it, and by the fact that no current speaker selects the next one. Let us now consider a third practice by which participants allocate the next turn.

What happens when neither of the two methods we have discussed is used to determine the next speaker? Sacks et al. (1978) say that if current speaker does not select the next one, and if no listener self-selects as next speaker, then (at the TRP) the current speaker may continue (p. 13). *Speaker continuation* is the technique by which a single participant may take an extended turn, but its use depends on the other two options not being used. Timing, as we said before, is critical if things are to go smoothly during turn allocation. In the two segments just above, we have seen instances of the current speaker electing to continue, where the current speaker's continuation was overlapped by a listener self-selecting (Segment 4.2, lines 1-2; Segment 4.3, lines 52-53). And the existence of the speaker-continues option is another reason for listeners to self-select quickly, for any delay may result in the current speaker resuming his or her turn.

Two other places in the "dark glasses" segment (4.3) are worth closer examination. It might seem from the written transcript that a TRP occurs at the end of line 49 (which would make lines 50-51 an instance of current speaker continues). On the tape recording, however, one can hear that B rushes on through "yesterday" and into "I might as well"; participants would most likely not project a TRP at the end of line 49. Lines 49-51 contain but a single turn construction unit. The other place is the short, untimed pause in line 56. This is not a TRP because "tha:t uh" indicates that J is not at the end of a turn construction unit and is not finished with his turn. So this, too, is not a case of current speaker continues, but is rather a case of a single turn construction unit. Finally, note that each of the three turn-allocation options applies again at the next TRP, and at the next, and so on.

The Sacks et al. (1978) model portrays conversational turn taking as *locally managed* and also *interactionally managed* by the participants (pp. 40-43). That is, it is the participants themselves, through the various practices they employ, who determine who shall speak next (and other important characteristics of turns, as we shall see). This management is local in the sense that it deals with the current turn and the impending next turn right at the point where speaker transition is relevant—the TRP. Turn allocation is not determined before participants begin (as in the case of the guitar recital), nor is it determined several turns ahead of time (as in standing in line at the ticket window). Conversational turn taking is interactionally managed in the sense that what one participant does affects what the others may acceptably do (for example, the use of current speaker selects next rules out other listeners self-selecting). Turn management is also interactional in the sense that the *possibility* that participants *can* do something affects how a participant may behave at the moment (for example, the possibility of the current speaker continuing affects how listeners use self-selection).

This locally, interactionally, participant-managed turn system—with its three turn-allocation practices operating at the TRP—is one of the defining characteristics of conversation. Other types of communication, other systems for exchanging talk, usually have their turn taking organized in ways different from that found in conversation. And the conversational system of turn taking has important consequences for how conversation unfolds, for how it is shaped and organized, and for how mistakes and other problems are dealt with.

☐ Consequences of the Turn System

The system of turn taking discussed above is closely connected to the organization or structure that unfolds as conversation progresses. In fact, the turn system is largely responsible
for several obvious structural characteristics of everyday conversation. It also provides students of conversation with an
analytical framework with which to examine these and other
characteristics of conversation. We begin with a consideration
of a few of the most obvious and observable facts.

GROSSLY APPARENT FACTS

Sacks et al. (1978) relate their turn-taking model to a list of
"grossly apparent facts" of conversation (pp. 10-11, 14-40). In
each case, they describe how the fact is a result of, or at least
compatible with, some feature(s) of the model. We shall review
five selected facts.

First, only one participant usually speaks at a time, and overlap, when it occurs, is brief. As we have seen, the turn system
localizes speaker change at the TRP. This means that instances
of coordination problems will generally cluster around specific
points in the flow of talk, points at which speakers will have
reached a possible completion. In addition, whichever participant is properly selected as next speaker is given exclusive
rights to the turn. That is, participants orient to resolving overlapping talk, usually by one person dropping out. On the other
hand, the encouragement given by the turn system for listeners
to self-select as early as possible results in instances of this brief
overlap being fairly common. By way of contrast, certain audience response modes (responsive reading, for example) in reli-
gious services or political meetings are organized so that a
single participant (the "leader") takes one turn, but the entire
audience responds together in the next turn.[2]

Second, the order and distribution of speaker turns is not
fixed or determined in advance, but varies within and between
conversations. The turn system allows this variation in who

speaks next, who speaks after that, who gets more turns, and who gets fewer by providing three options for how the next turn is allocated. Each of these options leads (potentially) to a different next speaker. For example, current speaker selects next leads to the current speaker's choice of the moment, while listener self-selection leads to whoever starts first at the TRP. This is a good example of a fact of conversation that results directly from the local management of turns. A nonconversational contrast to this is formal debate, in which the order of speakers is determined ahead of time, usually by the style of debate being performed. Even the number of times each participant speaks may be fixed in advance.

Third, the size or length of turns varies from one turn to the next. Two different aspects of the turn system contribute to this characteristic of conversation. Turns are constructed out of various size units in the first place. Words, phrases, clauses, and sentences are generally of different sizes, and each type of unit can vary in length as well (sentences can be long or short, for example). In addition, the option that current speaker can continue (if neither of the other options has been exercised) allows a speaker to lengthen his or her turn after the first turn construction unit. Again, this is a clear example of the effect of local management of turns. Debate again provides a good contrast, because the speeches of participants have a fixed maximum length (measured, say, in minutes and seconds).

Fourth, what participants say in their turns, or what actions they do with their turns, is not restricted or specified in advance. Of course, what participants may acceptably do in any particular turn is restricted by what happened in prior turns and by general social norms, but the turn system itself does not require that conversational turns be used only for certain types of actions or contain only certain types of information. Along with the local management of turns, this also is a defining characteristic of conversation. The turn systems of broadcast news interviews and courtroom direct and cross-examination of witnesses, in contrast, both operate under the restriction that one participant will use turns primarily to ask questions and other participants will primarily answer them. And in many ceremonies, the actual words participants must speak are scripted ahead of time. Note also that in some transcontinental telephone calls, participants routinely end their turns by saying some transition word, such as "over." This is a way of coping with the long time lag between the ending of one's turn and the first sound of the other's turn. Conversational turn taking does not depend on participants' saying anything special.

> *The very nature of everyday conversation derives from its turn-taking system.*

Finally, perhaps the most obvious fact about conversation (and again, a defining characteristic of it) is that speaker change occurs. The turn system provides for this through its two options for transferring to another speaker: current speaker selects next and listener self-selection. In addition, the turn system supplies periodic places at which speaker change can conveniently occur: the TRP at the end of each turn construction unit. Contrast this with both classroom lecturing and public speaking, in which speaker change may not occur, or may be restricted to a few places controlled by the lecturer ("Are there any questions?").

Thus the very nature of everyday conversation derives, in large part, from its turn-taking system. Its most noticeable characteristics are closely linked both to the ways in which turns are *constructed* (using words, phrases, clauses, sentences, and TRPs) and to the ways they are *allocated* (using the practices of current speaker selects next, listener self-selects, and current speaker continues). Even more important to the study of interpersonal communication, however, is the fact that many of the conversational tendencies and orientations that we commonly attribute to participants' personalities or interpersonal relationships derive (at least in part) from the turn system. For example, other participants may listen to us not because they are interested or because we are fascinating, but because they have to. We now examine several of these far-reaching consequences of turn organization in conversation.

MOTIVATION FOR LISTENING

Why do people listen to each other during ordinary conversation? Although it occasionally happens that someone is discovered not to have been listening, for the most part we listen to each other's everyday talk. One answer to the question might be that people are interested in what other participants have to say. While this may be true, it does not adequately account for why we listen, because we all listen to talk that we are not interested in. Another answer might be that we listen to maintain the interpersonal relationships we have with other participants (for example, we want to be polite). This answer is closer to the point, but fails to address the connection between our interpersonal relationships and how conversation is conducted. One connection lies in the turn system.

The organization of conversational turn taking provides "an intrinsic motivation for listening" (Sacks et al., 1978, pp. 43-44). During the current turn anyone can be selected by the speaker to be next. Participants who are willing to speak if selected— that is, who are not willing to be "caught napping" or to be found rude—must monitor the course of the current turn to discover whether they have been selected. Furthermore, participants who may want to self-select at the upcoming TRP— regardless of whether they intend to continue the ongoing discussion or change it radically—must monitor the current speaker's talk to determine whether anyone has been selected as next speaker. If a given listener has been selected to speak next, he or she must cope with responding to the current utterance; if a given listener has not been selected, he or she must still determine whether anyone else has been selected as next speaker, because, if so, self-selection is ruled out. So things that happen in the current turn are potentially vital to how we should conduct ourselves in the next turn, whether we should speak (and, if so, what we may appropriately say) or whether we should remain silent. Participants who do not wish to be called to account for violations of conversational norms have a reason for listening that stems from the turn system, independently of whether the speaker's talk is interesting in the broader sense.

COMPETITION FOR TURNS

Conversational turns are valued, sought after (and sometimes avoided, negatively valued). When the current speaker has not selected next, there is frequently competition for the next turn. We have seen that the rule giving exclusive rights to the earliest self-selecting listener contributes to this, but there is more involved. Why should a listener (who wants to talk) compete for the very next turn? That is, why not wait until other participants have had their say and then self-select when there is no competition for the turn? We occasionally do this, of course, but it is usually when what we have to say can be said anytime during the conversation. When participants wish to respond to, comment about, or elaborate on what the current speaker is saying, they strive to obtain the very next turn. Why should this be so? For one thing, participants interpret an utterance done in the very next turn as being relevant to the adjacently prior one, as we saw in Chapter 3. It is easier to show the relationship of one's talk to what the current speaker is saying if one can get the very next turn. But the constraint imposed by the turn system is also a major influence on turn competition. If a participant does not successfully self-select for the next turn, then whoever does become next speaker may select someone else as the following speaker; that person may select still another participant, and so on. The availability of the current speaker selects next technique means that a participant can *count* on his or her impending utterance being relevant to the ongoing talk *only* if it is done in the very next turn. After that, the conversation may take other directions not related to what he or she was going to say. This can be a major contributor to competition for turns.

TURN RESERVATION

A potential problem faced by conversational participants is that on occasion they may wish to take an extended turn (to tell a story, for example). The reason this could be a problem lies in a particular feature of the turn system. We have examined how a speaker has rights to the current turn up to the first TRP. That is, turns are allocated one turn construction unit at a time. A participant who wishes to produce an utterance several units long is subject to losing the turn at each TRP, where any listener may self-select. This leads to the common practice of using a turn to secure participants' agreement to allow the speaker to take an extended turn (or possibly an extended series of turns). Reserving the turn is a major function of the presequence (or at least the pre), which we looked at in Chapter 3.

Just as an adjacency pair sequence is often projected by an earlier sequence (the presequence), so larger structures of talk such as jokes, stories, and actions accompanied by background or other preparation are projected or announced in various prefaces or presequences. Stories and jokes, for example, are often announced, as in Data Segment 4.4.

(4.4) [Levinson, 1983, p. 323 (from Sacks)]
1 K: You wanna hear muh- eh my
2   sister told me a story last night.
3 R: I don't wanna hear it. But if you must.

K produces a story announcement and gets the go-ahead from R, although a somewhat reluctant one. After some banter among the participants, K then tells a fairly lengthy dirty joke. This use of the presequence serves other functions as well, such as ensuring that the speaker does not tell a joke or story that others have already heard. But a major function is temporarily to suspend competitive self-selection at TRPs and allow a speaker to work through an extended turn. In other cases, the speaker gets a series of turns, with some other participant briefly acknowledging each one. In his study of action projections, Schegloff (1980) notes that when people say something like "Can I ask you a question?" the next thing they typically produce is not the question, but some preliminary talk leading up to it. Data Segment 4.5 begins with B projecting that a question will be forthcoming (lines 1-2).

(4.5) [Schegloff, 1980, pp. 108-109, abbreviated]
```
 1  B:  Now listen, Mister Crandall, let
 2      me ask you this. A cab. You're
 3      standing onna corner. I heardjuh
 4      talking to a cab driver.
 5  A:  Uh::uh
 6  B:  Uh was it- uh was a cab driver,
 7      wasn' i'?
 8  A:  Yup,
 9  B:  Now, yer standing onna corner,
10  A:  Mm hm,
11  B:  I live up here in Queens.
12  A:  Mm hm,
            ((18 speaker turns omitted))
46  B:  Now is he not suppose' tuh stop fuh me?
```

In this case, B's action projection ("let me ask you this") is a pre that helps to secure a long series of turns leading up to the intended action (a question about when a cab is supposed to stop to pick up a customer). Throughout this series of turns, A produces continuers (such as "Mm hm") that occupy a turn in only a token way and return speakership to B (see Schegloff, 1982). B is thus able to lead up to and eventually produce the projected question without having to compete for the turn at each TRP. Notice that stories and other extended-turn structures in conversation are not simply produced by a single speaker, but are jointly or interactively produced by a primary speaker together with other cooperating participants (see, for example, Mandelbaum, 1987).

> *The place where a silence occurs is an important factor in how it gets treated.*

TREATMENT OF SILENCES

As students of conversation, we should not treat all conversational silences in the same way, in large part because participants do not either. The place where a silence occurs in the turn construction and allocation process is an important determining factor in how it gets treated. Sacks et al. (1978) distinguish among three different types of silence. One is the *lapse*, which occurs during and after a TRP, when the current speaker has not selected a next speaker, no listener has self-selected, and current speaker elects not to continue. That is, at the end of a turn, when no next speaker is selected through any of the three turn-allocation options, the conversation comes to an end—lapses—at least for the moment.

A second type of silence is the *gap*. This is a silence at the TRP (usually brief, often about one second or less) when the current speaker has not selected a next speaker and a self-selecting listener has not yet started. In other words, a gap is the silence between the end of one turn and some listener self-selecting for the next turn. In the "dark glasses" segment (4.3), the silence in line 55 is an example of this (despite its 2.6-second duration). We might think of this as a sort of reaction time, the time it takes a listener to "read" the TRP, generate something relevant to say, and begin talking. An important characteristic of the gap, however, is that it is not attributed to any specific participant (it does not "belong" to anyone). It is just the silence—the gap—between speakers.

The third type of silence is the *pause*. This is a silence within a participant's turn, a silence that is attributable to that person. Pauses arise in three primary ways. First, a speaker can produce a silence during the course of his or her turn. This version of the pause does not occur at a TRP and can be related to a variety of factors, from being momentarily distracted to searching for the right word. The short, untimed silence in line 56 of the "dark glasses" segment (4.3) is this sort of pause. Note that J's pause is short in part because he uses "uh" to fill some of the space between "tha:t" and "I." Second, a pause arises when, after a silence at the TRP, no listener self-selects and the current speaker elects to continue. The silence at the TRP then retrospectively becomes a silence *within* that speaker's turn—a pause. Third, a pause can occur when the current speaker selects a next speaker and, at the TRP, that person delays in responding. Line 2 in the "met Missiz Kelly" segment (4.1) is a case in point. After A selects B by asking a question (line 1), B delays a full second before speaking. Why is this type of silence a pause rather than a gap? Because it is attributable to the person selected as next speaker. In this example, B has rights and obligations to the turn effective immediately after A's turn ends (that is, at the TRP). Thus the silence in line 2 is considered B's silence—B's pause before speaking. As participants, we often treat pauses differently from gaps. We may attribute uncertainty or impending disagreement (as discussed in Chapter 5) to a selected next speaker's pause, for example, when we would not make such attributions to a speaker self-selecting after a gap.

Silence is an important component of everyday conversation. The interpretation that participants give to conversational
silence, as reflected in their subsequent utterances (or lack of
such utterances), depends on the location of the silence in the
turn-taking sequence. This is our justification for using three
different terms to name silences. The most critical distinction
is probably that between silences before a self-selecting listener
starts to speak and silences within an already selected speaker's
turn. Unfortunately, while this usage is standard among conversation analysts, it is not standard among many communication and other scholars who study interpersonal processes.[3]
Despite some problems in terminology, however, research has
rather consistently shown that perceptions of participants'
communicative competence and even the viability of their conversation is related to the way they manage conversational
silence (see, e.g., Cappella & Planalp, 1981; Wiemann, 1977).

BIAS IN TURN ALLOCATION

The turn system allows participants to allocate speaking
turns in very unequal or biased patterns. The newcomer to the
group, for example, may be favored with frequent selection as
next speaker by various current speakers. Someone in disfavor
may not be selected at all and may be able to speak only through
self-selection in competition with everyone else. Listeners may
choose not to self-select after the turns of a particularly powerful, esteemed, or interesting participant, thus allowing him or
her the option to continue. One of the most common patterns
(as noted by Sacks et al., 1978) is for the current speaker to select
the previous speaker to talk again. This pattern allows the
development of more extended dyadic structures of conversation, such as elaborated arguments, dialogues, or colloquies.

This possibility for bias in turn-taking patterns is a good
illustration of an important characteristic of Sacks et al.'s
(1978) model. The turn system is *context free*, yet it can be *context
sensitive* to a variety of particular conversational happenings
(p. 10). What this means is that the organization of turn taking

and the practices used to accomplish it do not depend on any particular types of participants, social situations, physical settings, and so on. None of the participants has to be (or is prohibited from being) a student, the mayor, or a staff member of the local telephone crisis line, for example. And the conversation does not have to occur (nor is it prohibited from occurring) just after class has ended, at city hall, or over the telephone. Conversation operates across a very broad spectrum of different types of people, purposes, locations, group sizes, and interpersonal relationships. In order to do this, its basic mechanisms must be context free in the sense just described. At the same time, however, participants can design their talk and allocation of turns for the people who are actually present (and how many), for why they are having the particular conversation, for what their interpersonal relationships are, and so forth. In this sense, the turn system is context sensitive.

These consequences of the turn system for conversation (and others we have not examined here) derive from the system's orderliness and the way it organizes turns at talk. Who gets more turns (and who gets fewer), who gets longer turns (and who gets shorter ones), why there is often competition for turns, why people often listen to conversation even when they are not really interested in what is being said, and why silences are meaningful to us in different ways are all related to the practices we use for constructing and allocating turns. But what makes the system orderly and what happens when its orderliness breaks down? We now turn to a consideration of these questions.

❏ Turn Taking as a Normative System

We have all experienced conversations during which some sort of turn-taking trouble occurred. When two listeners begin talking at the same time, one usually drops out. A participant who misreads a TRP and starts talking before the current speaker has finished may apologize for the "interruption." Such instances show us that participants attempt to follow some set of rules or norms in their turn taking and to let others know what they are doing. In general, conversation is orderly because the participants work to make it so. That is, participants routinely take steps to display to each other that their talk is orderly and that the conversation as a whole has been orderly. When this is called into question, participants take steps to restore orderliness. This is as true of turn taking as it is of other aspects of conversation. In fact, it is because participants make their turn taking orderly *for each other* that it can be seen as orderly by analysts and other observers. One of the ways in which this orderliness is displayed is through participants' attention to the rules of conversational turn taking.

ORIENTATION TO RULES

The turn system is a normative system. That means that participants orient to the observance of certain communication rules (see Shimanoff, 1980). In most cases, participants design their talk so that it can be seen to be in conformity to one or more norms of turn taking. For example, listeners not selected as next speaker (by the current one) normally remain silent at the TRP so that the person selected can exercise his or her rights to the turn. In some cases, when a participant's talk can be seen as violating a norm, the person will take steps to bring his or her behavior into observable conformity with the rules. This occurs, for example, when a current speaker, in electing to continue, overlaps with a self-selecting listener and immediately drops out, thus orienting to the self-selecting listener's rights to the turn. In other cases, participants may bring sanctions to bear on someone whose behavior they see as violative. For example, they may mention the rule, or request that the person's behavior change in certain ways. Of course, participants sometimes ignore apparent violations of turn-taking norms and the talk proceeds without further incident.

Data Segment 4.6 presents an example of one participant reacting to the observable norm violation of another. The participants are playing the game of Scruples, in which the person whose official Scruples turn it is presents some selected other player with an ethical dilemma to respond to. In this case, the question is: Would you tell the hostess of a dinner party that a corpulent guest sat in her antique chair and cracked it?

(4.6) [Aakhus, 1988, p. 42, modified]
```
1  T: Okay: Jim
2  J: (1.3) hm:
3  T: You are at a dinner party. (.)
4     And hear a distinct ⌜crack  (0.8) as a corpule-⌝
5  M:              Jim ⌞at a dinner party (.) nchhh⌟
6     (1.0)
7  T: Can you⌜ sh:ut. up.
8  J:        ⌞a distinct (1.0) ⌜a distinct what?
9  T:                         ⌞a dis- a distinct cra:ck
```

T's summons (in line 1) and J's answer (in line 2) establish that T will be asking J a Scruples question (and taking an extended turn to do it). Other participants do not self-select during J's 1.3 second pause, thus orienting to the rule that only J has rights to that turn (after current speaker has selected next). T then begins her next turn by again selecting J as next speaker (with "you"), relying partly on having named him in the earlier summons. In the context of reading a multipart Scruples question from a card, and having identified J as the intended recipient, T's TRP at the end of line 3 is allowed to pass by all participants. This shows their orientation to her rights to finish the Scruples question. She continues on with the next part of the question (in line 4) and is overlapped by M, who jokes about Jim being invited to a dinner party. Note that the overlap (marked by the brackets between the lines) clearly begins before T's pause, so even if we judge the silence to occur at a TRP, M's utterance begins *during* T's turn and can be seen as a violation of turn-taking norms. A more accurate interpretation might be that T has reserved (and been granted) an extended turn through the combination of the Scruples game context and the summons-answer sequence. T breaks off her utterance (in line 4), which shows an orientation to the norm that only one person should speak at a time in conversation. M and T finish at about the same time and a one-second silence follows. One way of interpreting this is that other participants are treating the turn as still T's turn and are withholding their talk, thus orienting to her rights to continue speaking. She does (in line 7), and produces a complaint against M. This displays her orientation to turn-taking norms and to M's line 5 as a violation. Notice the emphasis on "sh:ut. up." Finally, J's question in line 8 seeks clarification of just that part of the Scruples question that was overlapped. It shows J's orientation to his selection as next speaker, along with his obligation to attempt an answer: J is requesting a repeat of that part of the question he apparently did not hear but is still responsible for answering.

Participants use the term interruption in a variety of ways.

Displays of orientation to the rules may be produced as much for observers or overhearers as for the participants themselves. In Data Segment 4.7, *CBS Evening News* anchor Dan Rather and (then) Vice President George Bush are engaged in a combative "news interview." There have been many instances of overlapping talk prior to this point, but on this occasion Rather produces an account for the overlap, thus displaying to the television audience (and to Bush) his orientation to turn-taking norms.

(4.7) ["Rather/Bush 'Interview,' " 1988-1989, p. 321, modified]
```
126  R:  Mis,ter Vice President, you set thee::
                [                                 ]
127  B:        an' the who:le story has been      =
128       =  told to the congress.
             [                        ]
129  R:      you set the rules fer this  :: this talk here.=
130       =I didn't mean to step on your line there, .hhh
131       but you insisted that this be li::ve,
```

The overlap in lines 126-127 and 128-129 is accounted for as having been inadvertent ("I didn't mean to"), despite the fact that such overlaps have been and continue to be frequent throughout the entire episode.

Note our continuing use of the term *overlap* rather than *interruption*. This is related to a potential problem in the way that both participants and researchers describe such incidents in conversation, a problem we now address.

OVERLAPS AND INTERRUPTIONS

Participants in everyday conversation apparently use the term *interruption* in a variety of ways. For example, a current speaker might regard a listener's slightly premature self-selection (just prior to a TRP) as an interruption if it is critical or otherwise unsupportive of the speaker, but not an interruption if it is supportive. Or, if current speaker selects a next speaker who pauses before starting, participants might regard a third party's self-selection during that pause as an interruption even if no actual overlapping talk resulted. If participants in a discussion regard themselves as being on opposite sides of the issue, they may feel interrupted by overlapping talk. But if the conversation is a generally cooperative one among friends, they may not feel that overlapping talk is a violation of their turn-taking rights. The point is that *interruption*, used as a folk (or vernacular) term by ordinary members of society, seems related not only to conversational structure, but to such factors as whether the participants like or agree with each other. Some overlaps (and even some nonoverlaps) may be regarded as interruptions—violations of turn-taking norms and social etiquette—while other overlaps may not. Bennett (1981) discusses the notion of interruption: It is "an interpretive category which participants can make use of to deal with currently prevailing rights and obligations in actual situations" (p. 176). This variability in the use of the term can be a source of confusion in studies of conversation when researchers use *interruption* in the vernacular.[4] Drummond (1989) contends that the premature labeling of overlap as *interruption* serves to obscure what is actually going on for the participants, such as one person dominating another, or one trying to help another (pp. 163-164).

Used in one way, *overlap* refers to simultaneous talk that arises from the normal operation of the conversational turn system (where two or more participants in a single conversation end up talking at the same time). As the turn system makes clear, this can arise in several different ways. First, a listener can self-select prematurely (under the pressure of trying to be first, or by misreading the extent of the current turn, for example). This would normally occur within a syllable or two of the TRP.[5] Second, more than one listener could self-select at the same moment. This would also occur at the TRP. Third, a listener could self-select at the same moment that the current speaker elects to continue. Again, this type of simultaneous talk would cluster at the TRP. In each of these categories, overlap occurs (due to slight miscoordinations and the like), even though all participants are orienting toward compliance with turn-taking norms. We will also use the term *overlap* more broadly to refer to simultaneous talk in general, including what others would call interruption. Used in this way, it is the generic term for simultaneous talk. None of the cases just described, however, would be interruption in the technical sense.

Interruption is used here to refer to simultaneous talk that does not occur at or near a TRP (Schegloff, 1987b, p. 85, n. 5; 1988-1989, p. 239, n. 10). It involves the apparent violation of turn-taking norms, in contrast to simultaneous talk that results from participants' orientation to those norms (overlap). When one participant begins to talk at a point where another (the current speaker) is taking a turn but not yet approaching a TRP, we shall (in most cases) term the resulting simultaneous talk an interruption.

Data Segment 4.8, taken from the same *CBS News* interview as Data Segment 4.7, contains two instances of simultaneous talk.

(4.8) [Nofsinger, 1988-1989, p. 284]
11 R: let's talk about the record.
12   You say that we' ̣ve misrepresented your record ̣
13 B: ᴸLet's   talk   about   the   ful̦l record
14 R: Let's talk about the record if ̦we've ̦ misrepresented
15 B: ᴸ Yeh ᴶ
16 R: your record in any way (0.4) . . .

Just prior to this segment, Bush had complained that *CBS News* was not conducting the interview properly. Rather, in line 11, proposes his version of how their talk should proceed and immediately continues by noting Bush's earlier charge that CBS was misrepresenting his record on Iran / Contra. After Rather's second sentence is well started ("You say that we-") and well before the next possible TRP (which would be at the end of line 12), Bush interrupts with a correction to the way Rather had formulated what the focus of their talk should be (Nofsinger, 1988-1989; on correction, see Jefferson, 1987; Schegloff, Jefferson, & Sacks, 1977). Bush proposes that the interview should be about the *full* record. This instance of simultaneous talk does not result from Bush orienting to the rules of the turn system: His utterance begins too late to count as occurring in conjunction with the prior TRP (at the end of line 11) and too early to be a "premature" self-selection related to the upcoming TRP. Also, note that Rather's utterance seems to have been broken off (we expect him to continue on with a question for Bush) and that he then repeats all of the overlapped portion (lines 14 and 16). The observation that Rather stopped and then produced his utterance again is an additional reason for categorizing this instance as an interruption. Compare this to the next instance of simultaneous talk (in lines 14-15). Here, it is possible that Bush projects a TRP after the word "record"; such an utterance would be similar to Rather's line 11. Bush self-selects with "Yeh," but Rather continues right on. Bush has (perhaps) misread the design of Rather's utterance and projected a TRP where Rather did not place one. This miscoordination while

104EVERYDAY CONVERSATION

orienting to the rules of the turn system results in an overlap that is not an interruption. It is unclear whether Bush was merely acknowledging Rather's utterance at this point (producing a one-word turn) or whether "Yeh" was to be the first word of a larger turn construction unit. If it is the latter case, by not continuing his utterance, Bush does show an orientation to the norm that only one participant should speak at a time.

Distinguishing among various types of overlap (including interruptions) is important because participants make strategic and normative decisions on the basis of how overlap occurs and their interpretation of it. Overlap can be a tactic for dominating a conversation, but it can just as well be a tactic for showing vigorous support of a speaker. Participants with different conversational styles may have trouble coordinating their turn taking and may attribute sinister motives to each other when overlap occurs (Tannen, 1984). Continuing research is needed to sort out the various functions of overlap and the meanings that participants attribute to it.

A temporary solution to the problem of how to use the terms *overlap* and *interruption*, then, is to confine the latter to a narrow technical use. But there are still other unresolved problems of a similar nature, such as the question of what to call instances in which a pause in the current speaker's turn is occupied by a listener self-selecting, or where a listener completes a current speaker's turn, with no resulting simultaneous talk. *Interruption* is not nearly as useful a term for the analyst as it is for participants.

So the turn system in conversation is a normative system in the sense that participants orient to its rules—by designing their behavior so that it conforms, by sanctioning or demanding an account of behavior that seems not to conform, or by providing accounts for or initiating repairs of such behavior. We will examine the details of various types of conversational repair in Chapter 5.

❏ A Different Turn-Taking System

Throughout this book, we have occasionally used data segments involving talk that did not occur in ordinary, everyday conversation. For example, the "Bush/Rather" segments (4.7 and 4.8) are excerpts from what began as a broadcast news interview, and other data segments have been from courtroom testimony. This raises the question of how turn taking is managed in these nonconversational yet thoroughly interactional episodes. It turns out, at least for communication episodes that are not predominantly scripted in advance (such as formal ceremonies), that their turn systems are modifications of the one for conversation. Another way of putting this is that the turn system we have just examined provides a useful point of departure for analyzing the turn organization in courtroom testimony, public news conferences, business meetings, and the like. We shall now briefly examine the turn system of broadcast news interviews (relying primarily on Greatbatch, 1988) as a way of advancing our understanding of conversational turn taking.

One major difference between ordinary conversation and broadcast news interviews is that, in the latter, participants generally limit themselves to producing one of only two types of communicative actions: questions and answers. In ordinary conversation, participants' turns may generally be used for the production of virtually any type of communicative action or action sequence. The turn system places no restriction on what a turn may consist of or be used for (although, as we have seen, some constraints do arise as a result of participants' designing their utterances to "fit" with prior ones). So, for example, while the recipient of an invitation may be expected to orient toward producing an acceptance, rejection, or clarifying insertion, there is no general requirement in conversation that "first" turns be used for invitations (or any other action), or that "second" turns be used for acceptances (or any other action). In broadcast news interviews, however, interviewers are generally constrained to use their turns for the production of utterances that are (at least minimally) recognizable as questions, and interviewees systematically orient to using their turns for producing answers. This constraint on what type of action participants are expected to produce in their respective turns is called *turn-type preallocation* (Greatbatch, 1988). Questioning turns are preallocated to interviewers and answering turns to interviewees. While this may seem to be an obvious (one might even say "grossly apparent") characteristic of this kind of interview, it is accomplished through the use of several coordinating practices that are not so obvious. Interviewers, for example, routinely produce statements during their turns, but they design them so as to support and provide for an impending question. That question is normally designed to make use of the preceding statements as preliminary material (Greatbatch, 1988, pp. 407-409). So the part of an interviewer's talk that is not actually a question is produced as leading up to, or as being in the service of, the next question. Furthermore, as prospective recipients of impending questions, interviewees routinely withhold comment on these preliminary statements and begin their turns upon completion of a recognizable question (Greatbatch, 1988, pp. 409-413). Interviewees thus treat interviewers' statements as preliminary to questions. Participants also have ways of orienting to the utterances of interviewees as being answers. For example, when interviewees produce talk that is not responsive to a prior question, they often attach it to a recognizable answer in the same turn (Greatbatch, 1986). As a result of participants' orientation to this preallocation of turn types, both interviewers and interviewees tend to get more extended turns than in everyday conversation. There are other systematic differences between conversational and broadcast news interview turn taking, as well.

The same sort of analysis could be conducted on the turn systems of courtroom testimony (see Atkinson & Drew, 1979), small group meetings, presidential (White House) news conferences, and other interactive communication episodes. In each case, participants employ modifications of conversational turn-taking practices. This makes a great deal of sense if we remember that children learn initially to converse and to use the everyday system of turn taking. Only later do people begin to attend business meetings and listen to news conferences or news interviews. And even though they may never solicit, give, or hear testimony in court, they would likely be competent participants in such activities, due to their conversational competence. As mentioned in Chapter 1, this is one of the things that makes the study of conversation so fundamental to understanding other forms of talk.

❏ Summary

The conversational turn-taking system is a major source of orderliness in everyday talk. From the perspective of the Sacks et al. (1978) model, turns are constructed using any of several different size units: words, phrases, clauses, and sentences. The possible completion point of a turn, the TRP (transition relevance place), can be projected by participants, who then employ three basic practices for allocating the next turn to someone. These practices are current speaker selects next, any listener self-selects, and current speaker continues. The transfer of speakership occurs at the TRP. The turn system operates the way it does because participants treat it as normative; that is, they orient to certain rules and treat certain behaviors as departures from (violations of) those rules. When such departures occur, participants work toward restoring orderliness. The operation of this turn system generates several patterns or tendencies in turn-taking behavior. Since failing to get the next turn when one wants it could result in not being able to produce one's utterance when it is most relevant, some competition for turns arises at TRPs. Certain types of overlaps and silences cluster around the TRP as well, although other types occur (with less frequency) away from the TRP. These patterns, and certain kinds of bias as to which participants get to speak more often and more extendedly, are closely related to the details of the turn system. Before we decide that "hogging the conversation," "not getting a word in edgewise," "being interrupted," "missing your turn," "finishing what someone was going to say before he or she said it," "getting your point across," "being a courteous conversationalist," and "having an interested conversational partner" are due to the personalities of the participants or the relationships among them, we need to examine closely how turn taking is being managed and what implications that has for the conduct of that particular conversation. Sacks et al. (1978) provide a practical model with which to work, although other models of conversational turn taking are available (see Wilson, Wiemann, & Zimmerman, 1984).

The picture that emerges from our study of turn organization in conversation is that of moment-by-moment coordination practices through which the participants themselves locally determine who shall speak next (and a variety of other characteristics of conversation). An episode of talk turns out to be a conversation (or a classroom discussion, or a news interview) partly because participants orient to the turn-taking rules of that particular form of talk. Note that we are not saying that certain rules or norms are somehow activated and then somehow "cause" participants to produce a conversation. On the contrary, it is the repeated demonstration by participants that they are orienting to a particular set of norms (out of a sense that others expect them to, or for whatever reason) that makes an episode recognizable to us as a conversation. Indeed, one of the interesting things about the Rather/Bush episode (from which Data Segments 4.7 and 4.8 are taken) is that it begins as a news interview and gradually becomes something like a conversational argument (see Clayman & Whalen, 1988-1989; Schegloff, 1988-1989). The set of practices through which turn coordination is achieved, however, is not the only respect in which participants display to each other what they are doing and what they mean. Conversations are cooperatively brought to a close, mistakes are repaired, and understandings are checked. Although these and similar processes are often treated separately in the conversation-analytic literature, we will group them together under the general term *alignment*. This is the topic of Chapter 5.

❏ Notes

1. Sacks et al. (1978) do not describe the mechanisms by which participants recognize these possible turn completion places (TRPs). Cues that function as turn yielding, and other turn-related signals, have been discovered by Duncan and his colleagues. Many of these are nonverbal, such as changes in voice pitch and termination of gestures. See Duncan (1972, 1973), McLaughlin (1984, pp. 99-103), and Wiemann (1985).

2. Note that even this sort of turn organization does not seem like such a great departure from that of ordinary conversation if we think of turns being taken not by an individual person, but by a *party* to the communication episode. In the case of mass audience participation, one party is the leader and the other party is the entire audience. In fact, Sacks et al. (1978) do not generally speak of people or participants, but rather say that the turn system allocates turns to parties.

3. The term *hesitation pause* is sometimes used for silences within one speaker's turn (whether at a TRP or not) and *switching pause* for silences between different speakers. McLaughlin (1984, pp. 111-122) provides a good discussion of these usages. *Switching pause* often equates to one of the three terms discussed above, but it may also involve elements of several different types of silences (including gaps and pauses). *Lapse* is sometimes used to mean a relatively long gap at the TRP, regardless of whether the talk that follows indicates that the conversation (or at least the topic) actually ended. McLaughlin and Cody (1982), for example, use a three-second minimum in defining *lapse* for their study. And since they wanted to examine the relationship between these long silences and the talk that follows, they avoided defining the lapse in terms of the following sequence. But from the perspective of the Sacks et al. (1978) model of conversational turn taking, the failure of anyone to self-select should be thought of as a gap if talk resumes "just where it left off" (with an utterance designed as a sequentially next turn to the last one, for example), but should be considered a lapse if talk resumes in a way that restarts (rather than continues) the conversation.

4. The issue has become important because interruption, operationalized in various ways, is thought to be a factor in dominance and gender effects in communication (see, for example, Dindia, 1987; Kennedy & Camden, 1983). Researchers have been using increasingly sophisticated definitions of interruption in recent years, incorporating such elements as the distance from a TRP

that an overlap begins and whether the overlapping talk is facilitative (support-ive) of the utterance it overlaps (West & Zimmerman, 1983). Although the beginning, termed the *onset*, of overlap is often used as a criterion for determin-ing interruption, some studies include the end or resolution of overlap as a criterion as well. Roger and Schumacher (1983), for example, distinguish be-tween successful and unsuccessful interruptions on the basis of whether "the first speaker was prevented from completing an utterance by the second speaker's taking the floor" (p. 702). Another procedure involves coding various characteristics of pre- and postinterruption talk as well as characteristics of the "interrupting" talk itself (Dindia, 1987; Kennedy & Camden, 1983). Drummond (1989) presents an excellent discussion of the shortcomings of these approaches, arguing that they are not sufficiently sensitive to the microdetails of how overlap actually occurs. One possible solution to this problem would be for analysts simply to give up using the term and to devise new terms or descrip-tions based (for example) on the word *overlap*. A similar solution, adopted by many conversation analysts, is to restrict *interruption* to a narrow technical use and not give it the broad range of interpretation it has in everyday parlance. Instances of overlap that both do and do not meet this narrow interpretation then receive descriptive accounts of their status. This is the practice adopted in this book.

5. See West and Zimmerman (1983, pp. 104, 113-114, n. 4) for a discussion of one way to distinguish overlaps from interruptions operationally.

5

Alignment

It is often critically important that we understand each other's talk. We are all painfully aware of the potentially embarrassing or tragic consequences of a conversation "gone wrong." At the beginning of Chapter 1, we noted that conversation is usually carried out successfully. People normally understand each other and the flow of talk is relatively orderly. Yet, we know that problems do arise: Participants occasionally misunderstand each other's actions, they misspeak and mishear, they forget a word or lose track of what was being said, they anticipate that a conversational action they wish to perform might be misunderstood, and so on. We also know that when problems arise, they are quickly taken care of. Conducting conversation often seems effortless, but it turns out that participants are successful because they actually work at it.

This chapter is about some of the processes that keep conversation "on track." Stokes and Hewitt (1976) refer to these processes as "aligning actions": "largely verbal efforts to restore

or assure meaningful interaction in the face of problematic situations . . . activities such as disclaiming, requesting and giving
accounts . . . offering apologies, formu-
lating the definition of the situation,

Participants
achieve interaction
by aligning their
individual actions.

and talking about motives" (p. 838). In
their essay, Stokes and Hewitt distinguish two senses of alignment. The one
they focus on is the process of resolving discrepancies between people's conduct and cultural expectations. Note
how the list of verbal procedures in
the quotation above (apologies, talking about motives, and so
on) is directed toward people's perceptions of what kind of
person the speaker is, toward managing one's social identity
when one may have violated cultural expectations. This sense
of alignment has received some attention in the communication
and sociology literature, particularly actions such as accounts
and disclaimers (see, for example, Buttny, 1985, 1987; Heritage,
1988; Hewitt & Stokes, 1975; Morris, 1985; Morris & Hopper,
1980; Mura, 1983; Scott & Lyman, 1968). It will not, however, be
our focus here. We will primarily consider "talk used to frame
messages for purposes of clarifying, interpreting, and managing conversational meaning and communicator roles" (Ragan,
1983, p. 159). The center of our attention will be on those activities through which participants achieve *inter*action by aligning
their individual actions. Notice the metaphor here: Different
participants' utterances and conversational actions are lined
up, straightened out, rectified, or laid out in an orderly way.
Participants can then achieve intersubjective understandings
rather than separate understandings; they can interact rather
than merely act. This is Stokes and Hewitt's (1976, pp. 838,
842-844) other sense of alignment.

In this chapter, we examine a wide variety of conversational
practices, from recipients' routine responses, to repairs of conversational problems, to preemption of another's turn, and more.
We thus are interpreting the term *alignment* very broadly, including in this chapter matters that might otherwise be treated

under quite separate categories. We begin with those second actions (second pair parts, adjacently placed utterances, and the like) that display an interpretation of the preceding action.

❑ Responses

Most conversations end with the participants feeling that they have understood each other. In most cases, later events prove this impression to have been correct. How do we achieve this, given that we do not (for the most part) explicitly ask each other whether we understand? In Chapter 3, we learned that certain types of conversational actions—first parts of adjacency pairs—make a set of second actions relevant in an especially powerful way. A second pair part is, in a sense, a response required by the normative orientation of the participants. Looking at the conversation backwards in time, the occurrence of a second pair part is evidence that its speaker is interpreting a prior utterance (not necessarily the immediately prior or adjacent one) in a particular way. The occurrence of an acceptance (or a rejection!), for example, can be taken as evidence that the speaker is orienting to another participant's utterance as having been an offer, an invitation, or some other related action.[1] This is one of the more obvious indications of how participants align to each other.

We have also seen that even when two actions do not have an adjacency pair relationship to each other, an action in the following turn—an adjacent second action—is normally regarded as a response to, or acknowledgment of, the first action. This is routinely the case unless that second action is somehow designed to warn participants not to interpret it that way. As a response, that second turn indicates something of how its speaker is interpreting the prior turn and thus what the alignment is between the two speakers. These points are illustrated in Data Segment 5.1.

(5.1) [Drummond, 1989, p. 159, modified]
38   P: O:h that's what I really need is a lid.
39   G: For your cake pan?
40   P: Ye:s, . . .

Let us assume for the moment that P's line 38 is a statement,
a sort of offhand remark of something that has occurred to her.[2]
Since it would not be a first pair part (not part of an adjacency
pair), it might occasion a wide variety of actions in the next
turn. G's utterance displays a particular interpretation of P: that
the lid referred to is a cake-pan lid. It also suggests that G wants
to have that interpretation confirmed (the upward inflection of
G's voice pitch may contribute to this). Notice that alternative
utterances in place of line 39 could display different understandings on the part of G. For example, "They're over in the
next aisle" might show that G knows what kind of lid P is
referring to and also that G interprets P as needing help locating
the right section in the supermarket. In any case, such an
adjacent utterance will provide P with evidence of the understanding G has of line 38—that is, with initial evidence of how
they are aligned to one another. P's response to G (line 40)
provides further evidence of their alignment. "Yes" displays P's
acceptance of G's understanding of what "a lid" means; they
appear to be well aligned on that matter. In addition, "yes"
treats G's utterance as a request for confirmation and thus
displays what sort of adjacency pair P takes lines 39-40 to be.
So adjacently placed second actions, as well as second pair
parts, convey to other participants (and to observers) a sense of
how that second speaker interprets the prior utterance. This
provides a preliminary basis for judging the extent to which
those two speakers are aligned. While this may be easy to see
as a general principle, careful analysis is needed to discover
exactly which conversational markers, devices, or practices are
used to display exactly what sorts of alignment. We now examine a number of specific responses through which participants
work toward alignment.

ASSESSMENTS

One type of prior action or utterance with which recipients routinely display alignment is the delivery of information. In Chapter 2 we discussed assertives, which would include most instances of statements, reports, announcements, and other types of information delivery. What we did not mention there is that participants often treat information delivery as conveying good news or bad news; they commonly use *assessments*—evaluative utterances—to indicate this alignment or interpretation (Heritage, 1984a, p. 302). Data Segment 5.2 shows an assessment used as a response to a delivery of information (more specifically, to a report solicited by a question).

(5.2) [Heritage, 1985, p. 96]
1 C: How's yer <u>foot</u>.
2 A: Oh it's healing beautifully:
3 C: <u>Goo::</u>d.

The report on A's foot (line 2) sounds like good news, but notice that it is not inevitably so. Perhaps A wants to stay out of school (or home from work) for a few more days, but now will no longer have the damaged foot as a reason. Whatever the situation, line 3 shows that C is responding to A's report as good news. This displays one particular alignment, one understanding of A's utterance. If we had A's *next* utterance, we would have evidence about A's response to C's assessment, evidence about their *mutual* alignment.

NEWSMARKS AND "OH" RECEIPTS

Recipients of announcements, reports, and the like, may also respond in a way that orients toward the informative value, sometimes even the surprise value, of the information delivery. Two conversational devices used to do this are the *newsmark* and the *"oh" receipt*. Gail Jefferson's concept of the newsmark is extensively described by Heritage (1984a, pp. 339-344, n. 13).

Newsmarks are words or other expressions "that specifically treat a prior turn's talk as news for the recipient rather than merely informative" (p. 340). They include expressions of surprise ("really?" "my goodness") and partial repeats of the prior turn ("she did?"), often with a pre-positioned "oh" ("Oh really?" "Oh did she?"). Since they stress the prior utterance's newsworthiness or surprise value for the recipient, newsmarks usually lead to further talk about the news item by the deliverer of the news, the recipient (producer of the newsmark), or both. In other words, newsmarks tend to align both participants to the continued need or appropriateness of further talk about that news, as shown in Data Segment 5.3.

(5.3) [Heritage, 1984a, p. 341]
1 E: They <u>charge</u> too much Guy,
2 G: Oh do they?
3 E: Yeh <u>I</u> think so,
4 G: What do they <u>cha</u>:rge.

G's newsmark (line 2) is designed as an "oh" plus a partial repeat. It leads to continued conversation about what was mentioned in E's delivery of information (line 1). The details of how a newsmark is designed seem to affect the direction of the talk that follows, such as what gets talked about and by whom (Heritage, 1984a, pp. 340-343).

It also turns out that "oh" is used in a variety of ways to show receipt of information (see the excellent analysis by Heritage, 1984a). Occasionally it is used alone, but usually it is combined with a newsmark or some other unit. Heritage proposes that such a use of "oh" functions as a change-of-state token, displaying that its user has changed from an *un*informed participant to an *informed* one on the basis of what someone else said in the previous turn. In this way, an "oh" receipt not only shows a new alignment between the deliverer of the information and its recipient (both are now informed about the matter), but also confirms the previous alignment that was the basis of the information delivery itself: The informer was knowledgeable and the recipient, previously, was not. Data Segment 5.4 contains two instances.

(5.4) [Heritage, 1984a, p. 301, modified]
1 J: Hello there I rang y'earlier but chu wur ou:t,
2 K: <u>Oh:</u> I musta been at <u>D</u>ez'z m<u>u</u>:m's=
3 J: =Oh::.

J informs K of an earlier phone call (line 1). Notice that the assumption of K's ignorance of this matter is almost verbalized here ("but chu wur ou:t"). In the next turn, K's response combines an "oh" receipt with an account of why K had failed to answer the phone. The "oh" receipt proposes that K had previously been unaware of J's call, but is now informed. The account itself includes an information delivery (with J as the intended recipient) and thus proposes that J is uninformed about the facts it conveys. J's response (line 3) is also an "oh" receipt, displaying that J was indeed unaware of K's whereabouts, but has now become informed about the matter. Both participants not only align themselves to their newly changed states, but display their previous states as well. Various types of newsmarks and "oh" receipts may affect the subsequent conversation in different ways. Detailed analysis is needed to determine what importance these differences may have for the conduct of conversation.

CONTINUERS

The effect of newsmarks and "oh" receipts can be more thoroughly appreciated by contrasting them to a superficially similar set of conversational markers or devices with a quite different function. We are all aware that recipients of another person's talk frequently respond with short vocalizations such as "mm hmm," "uh huh," and "yeah." Except when these utterances occur after yes/no questions (where they are taken to be a yes answer), they are usually identified in communication classes as feedback or back-channel behaviors (a term used by Duncan & Fiske, 1977, and others). The claim is usually that "listeners" use these responses to display to the speaker that they are paying attention, listening, and perhaps even understanding. This would seem to place such responses in almost the same category as newsmarks and "oh" receipts. Schegloff (1982), however, reminds us that a great many responses display that the person producing them is listening to, and has some sort of understanding of, the prior speaker. Many utterances would display this better than "uh huh" (pp. 78-79). Clarification questions and statements of disagreement, for example, are usually clearer indications of listener attention and understanding than "mm hmm." We have seen that what is special about "oh" receipts and newsmarks is that they display the informational and news value of the prior turn. What, then, is really special about utterances such as "uh huh" and "yeah"?

By saying something like "uh huh," participants avoid taking a full turn.

In Chapter 4, we noted that conversational turns are constructed out of several types of units (words, phrases, clauses, and sentences). We also discovered that turns are constructed one unit at a time, in the sense that each unit is followed by a TRP at which the current turn may be brought to an end. With the cooperation of all participants, however, multiunit turns may be constructed. What this requires is that listeners *not* self-select as next speaker at the TRP (and, of course, that current speaker not select next). The current speaker may then continue and produce a multiunit turn. Schegloff (1982) argues that recipients of a potentially multiunit turn produce "mm hmm," "uh huh," "yeah," and so forth as *continuers*. That is, by saying something like "uh huh," participants avoid taking a full turn at talk. They also display their understanding that the other speaker is building an extended turn and should continue with the next unit of it (pp. 80-81). It is also important to recognize that different tokens (say, "mm hmm" versus "yeah") may function somewhat differently as continuers.

C. Goodwin (1986) has shown that continuers that overlap an ongoing utterance often overlap the end of one turn unit and the beginning of another, acting as a sort of "bridge" between parts of a multiunit turn (pp. 207-208). Consider Data Segment 5.5 as a case in point.

(5.5) [C. Goodwin, 1986, p. 206, modified]
1 H: One time I member, .hh 's girl wrote
2   and her, .hh she wz like (.) fifteen er
3   six,teen   and her mother doesn' let'er wear
4 N: ⌈Uh hu:h,⌉
5 H: .hh nail polish . . .

N's continuer in line 4 allows her to avoid taking a full turn herself just at the point where H is finishing one turn construction unit (" . . . she was like fifteen or sixteen") and beginning another ("and her mother doesn't let her wear nail polish . . . "). N thus displays both her recognition that H is involved in producing a multiunit turn and her cooperation in allowing H to continue. In so doing, N aligns with H's role of the moment as the primary producer of substantive turns. Continuers, then, are indeed alignment devices. But they display alignment to the *type* of turn another speaker is producing rather than to the newsworthiness or informational value of that turn. (Their use also differs in important ways from that of assessments, according to Goodwin.)

Having distinguished the operation of continuers from newsmarks, we should now recognize that research on the alignment function of these responses is not complete, and that things are more complicated than we have portrayed. For example, there is a conversational environment, a context, in which partial repeats (which we have classified as newsmarks) and continuers seem to function similarly. Recipients of an extended set of instructions or directions over the telephone often use partial repeats and continuers to mark the successful receipt of an instruction and to return speakership to the participant giving the instructions (see, for example, Goldberg, 1975). Data Segment 5.6 involves the delivery of directions about how to get to a particular address; Data Segment 5.7 is from a radio talk show in which a listener is getting instructions about how to make a cheesecake. Both are types of information delivery.

(5.6) [Psathas, 1986, p. 245]
  5 A: get on the Free:way,
  6 C: mm hmm,
  7 A: an get off at Burbank Boulevard.
  8 C: mm hmm,
  9 A: head toward the mountains,
 10 C: mm hmm,

(5.7) [Goldberg, 1975, p. 271, modified]
  1 D: Now that's yur crust, and then you press it
  2   into a ten inch spring pan t' form the crust.
  3 S: Oka:y.
  4 D: Now intuh a large mixing bowl
  5   y'beat those four eggs,
  6 S: Beat eggs.
  7 D: Until they're light 'n' fluffy
  8 S: Mhm
  9 D: An now you break in the cream
 10   chee:se ⌈bit   ⌈by bit,=
 11 S: ⌊Break in the cream ⌊cheese
 12 D: =Y'know little mouthful atta time.

C's responses in Data Segment 5.6 function as continuers because they lead to A taking an immediate next turn and producing the next piece of the directions. But they also seem to display that C interprets A's directions as adequate, as being suitably informative (Psathas, 1986, p. 235). In that sense, they function somewhat like change-of-state markers. In Data Segment 5.7, S's responses in lines 3 and 8 work that same way, and the partial repeats in lines 6 and 11 also serve both to mark adequate understanding or receipt of the instruction (they function like newsmarks) and to occasion D's production of the next part of the instructions (as a continuer would). These types of responses display the way in which a recipient of information is aligned to some of the details of the turn that delivers the information.

FORMULATIONS

Another alignment device that can be distinguished from the partial repeat is the *formulation*. On occasion, a participant will summarize or give the gist of what some other participant(s) said (see Heritage & Watson, 1979, 1980). Whether this is done as an immediate response to a single prior utterance or as a delayed summary of a broader stretch of prior talk, the person who formulates what somebody else said is displaying a certain understanding of that earlier talk. This is an important source of alignment in everyday conversation and other types of interactive talk.[3] Heritage (1985), in analyzing their use in broadcast news interviews, reminds us that formulations are not necessarily comprehensive or neutral summaries of prior talk. They often "re-present" only a narrow selection from what had been said, or propose the "upshot" or further significance of a prior speaker's talk. In Data Segment 5.8, a woman who has won a dieting award (the "Slimmer of the Year") is being interviewed.

(5.8) [Heritage, 1985, p. 101]
```
 1  S:  . . . I never ever felt my age or looked my age,=I was
 2       always (.) older,=people always took me for older. .hhhh
 3       And when I was at college I think I looked a ma:tronly
 4       fifty. .hh And (.) I was completely alone one weekend
 5       and I got to this stage where I almost jumped in the
 6       river(hh).=I just felt life wasn't worth it anymo:re,
 7       =it hadn't anything to offer (.) .hhhh and if this was
 8       living I had had enough.
 9  I:  You really were prepared to commit suicide because
10       you were a big fatty.
11  S:  Yes, 'cuz I- I (.) just didn't see anything in life that
12       I had to look forward to . . .
```

The interviewer's formulation in lines 9-10 selectively focuses on some aspects of S's utterance, ignores others, renames her

contemplated action (as suicide), and elaborates on the relationship between that action and her weight (Heritage, 1985,
pp. 101-104). Thus a formulation displays its speaker's alignment in the sense that it exhibits not only what he or she
understands from a prior turn, but what is proposed as important to focus on, clarify, confirm, and so forth. Formulations
routinely occasion the action of confirming/disconfirming in
the next turn (as in lines 11-12 above), thereby providing evidence of the state of mutual alignment between the participants. This is a skill (usually called *summarizing*) that we often
explicitly teach in small group and interpersonal communication courses. The assumption is that perhaps the best way to
align one's understanding with what someone else intended to
convey is to formulate that other participant's talk and monitor
his or her response.

COLLABORATIVE COMPLETIONS

Another conversational device that displays alignment between participants is the *collaborative completion*. In contrast to
formulations, communication skills courses generally do not
teach collaborative completions. On the contrary, we may even
discourage their use, treating them as a form of "interruption"
(recall the difficulty we had pinning down that concept in
Chapter 4). Lerner (1989, p. 173) provides a brief description of
collaborative completion, although the extensive analysis he
has done on this phenomenon has not yet been published (see,
e.g., Lerner, 1987). Data Segment 5.9 illustrates a collaborative
completion and the response to it by the first speaker.

(5.9) [Lerner, 1989, p. 173, modified]
1 R: If you bring it in tuh them
2 C: it don't cost yuh nothing

Overly simplified, Lerner's argument is this: The organization or syntax of certain utterances is in two parts, and the
occurrence of the first component allows other participants to

project what the second component might be. The recipient can then preemptively complete the first speaker's utterance. For example, in an utterance with the components "if X" and "then Y," the production of the first component, "if X," by one participant allows other participants to project what the second component might be and to produce "then Y" before the first speaker does. In the data segment above, R's line 1 is designed as an "if X" component (X, in this case, being "you bring it in tuh them"). From this, C is able to project that R's utterance can be completed with a "then Y" clause, the Y being "it don't cost yuh nothing." Note that "then" is often not crucial to the sense of the collaborative utterance and (as in this instance) may not actually be spoken. C's preemptive completion of R's turn indicates the nature of C's alignment with R's talk. It also makes relevant an acceptance or rejection in the next turn (p. 173). Alternative completions are possible, of course (for example, "they'll have it ready the next day"), so the response by the first speaker is important to assessing the extent of the participants' mutual alignment. A "yeah" or some other acceptance by R of C's collaborative completion would display that C was closely aligned to both the substance and the structure (the two-component format) of R's talk.

To summarize, in addition to the second parts of adjacency pairs, most next or adjacent actions display how the speakers who produced them have interpreted prior talk. Newsmarks and "oh" receipts display that the prior talk was newsworthy, while assessments show the speaker's evaluation of that information as good or bad. Formulations are used by a participant to display his or her version of the gist or upshot of prior talk. Collaborative completions show the second or completing speaker's sense of both the organization and the substance of the other participant's utterance. But continuers, contrary to common belief, do not function primarily to display a participant's understanding of the prior utterance. Instead, they indicate a participant's expectation that the other speaker will continue on to produce an extended turn and they display cooperation in allowing that other speaker to do so. Through

these and other related practices, participants continually re-
fresh their intersubjective understandings of the course of the
conversation and renew their alignment with each other.

Although the types of responses we have examined here form
the foundation of an ongoing process of revealing and updating
the alignment between participants, they do not all perform
exactly the same work. The rich variety and subtle detail of
these aligning responses would be lost if we were simply to
classify them into some convenient category, such as "acknowledgments." A related set of processes that is crucial to the
maintenance and restoration of alignment is repair, which can
involve one, two, or even three turns at talk.

❏ Repair

Conversation, like other forms of human behavior, is not
perfect. Everyone has experienced forgetting a word or using
the wrong one, starting a sentence and then having to start over,
realizing that what has been said is unclear, and the like. It is
important for our understanding of each other that we fix these
flaws before they lead to more serious and fundamental problems. Participants routinely make various sorts of errors and
then either revise what they have said or have the problems
rectified by other participants. Participants also let noticeable
errors go unrectified and revise talk that seems to have no
noticeable errors! The general technical name for the processes
through which we fix conversational problems (or, in some
cases, nonproblems) is *repair.*

It comes as no surprise to us that conversational repair is a
major source of alignment between participants. Schegloff et al.
(1977) have specified several important distinctions that we
should attend to. One is the distinction between the *initiation* of
repair (that is, noticing or marking a source of trouble) and the
outcome of the process (the resulting changes), which we will
simply call *repair.* A second distinction concerns who produces

the actual initiation or repair. When the speaker who produced the trouble source (which is sometimes called *the repairable*) also produces the initiation or repair, we shall refer to it as *self-initiation* or *self-repair*; when some other participant does, we shall call it *other-initiation* or *other-repair* (Schegloff et al., 1977, pp. 362-365). Data Segments 5.10 and 5.11 indicate some of the variety of conversational practices that constitute repair.

(5.10) [Frankel, 1989, p. 214]
8 P: She tasted it? is it l- in a liquid for:m?
9 C: Ye:s

(5.11) [Off-con, KC, modified]
((C knocks, B invites C to come in, C enters the office))
1 B: Why don'cha flick on the lights. (0.9)
2   I've (0.6) discovered th't (0.3) I'm in the dark
3   (0.9)
4 C: hhuh .hh
5 B: hh .hh Which actually is: (0.6)
6   an enlightening experience
7 C: hh heh heh heh
8   .hh t' discover it? or t'be.
9 B: t' discover it.

In Data Segment 5.10, C has called a poison control center to get information about a substance that her daughter has "tasted." P, a staff member at the center, asks a clarifying question in line 8 and seems to be going to say "is it liquid." But P breaks off the sentence after the "l" sound and changes to "in a liquid form." This is a self-initiated self-repair. P produces the trouble source and marks it as problematic by breaking off after the first sound of a word. This is the self-initiation. Then P immediately produces what appears to be an alternative expression. This is the self-repair. Notice that this is one of those instances where there is no clear error or mistake in the utterance that we have called the *trouble source*. It seems that "is it liquid" is just as correct as "is it in a liquid form." Not all trouble sources exhibit actual trouble, even though they get repaired.

In Data Segment 5.11, C has just entered B's office, which was lighted only by the daylight coming in the window. B (who had been in the office eating his lunch) asks C to flip on the lights and then jokes about having been "in the dark." B's next comment (lines 5-6) proves problematic for C and leads to an other-initiated self-repair. C requests clarification in line 8. This is the other-initiation. That is, the trouble source is B's, but it is marked as troublesome by C. B then provides clarification (line 9) of his own earlier utterance; this is the self-repair. Schegloff et al. (1977, pp. 363-365) say that either type of initiation can result in either type of repair or in a failed repair, as when one speaker is searching for a word or name and the other cannot remember it either. Successful repair—and thus improved alignment—is often a joint accomplishment of the participants.

Repairs are overwhelmingly done in close proximity to the trouble source.

SEQUENTIAL POSITIONING

Repairs are overwhelmingly done in close proximity to the turn containing the trouble source. As participants' talk moves away from a problematic turn, it becomes more and more difficult to design an effective repair. In those instances where a much earlier utterance is belatedly discovered to have been a trouble source, we would expect that a more elaborate repair would be required, since the specific turn containing the trouble source, as well as the nature of the trouble, would have to be displayed. These matters are simplified when the repair is done immediately.

Initiations and repairs by the same speaker who produced the trouble source routinely occur in one of three sequential positions: They occur in the same turn as the trouble source, as in the "liquid form" segment (5.10 above); they occur at the TRP following that turn; and they occur in the third turn (speaker's next turn after recipient's response), as the repair does in the "in the dark" segment (5.11) (Schegloff et al., 1977, p. 366). Data Segment 5.12 illustrates a repair accomplished in the TRP space after the trouble-source turn.

(5.12) [Schegloff et al., 1977, p. 370]
1 B: . . . then <u>more</u> people will show up.
2   Cuz they won't feel obligated tuh sell.
3   tuh buy.

The end of line 2 is the end of a turn construction unit (remember that the period indicates a downward voice inflection). But before another participant begins to speak, B extends the turn with another unit designed as a replacement for the last phrase in that would-have-been-completed turn (a replacement for "tuh sell"). Notice that the adjacent placement of "tuh buy," as well as its parallel design, both identifies it as a repair and locates the specific trouble source. This data segment is also an example of a specific subcategory of repair. When the repair consists merely of substituting or replacing an item with another item, it is often called *correction* (Schegloff et al., 1977, p. 363). Close proximity, then, links the repair to the trouble source in this case just as it does in the "liquid form" segment (5.10).

Self-repair in the third turn can result from other-initiation (as the "in the dark" segment shows), but it can also follow self-initiation in that same third turn. Data Segment 5.13 is an example of this.

(5.13) [Jefferson, 1987, p. 86]
1 H: And he's going to make his own paintings.
2 B: Mm hm,
3 H: And- or I mean his own frames,
4 B: Yeah,

H's first turn (line 1) is responded to with a continuer by B (the second turn). In the third turn, H breaks off after the first word (an indication of some sort of trouble) and produces a correction of the first turn: "Paintings" is changed to "frames." We see in these self-initiations and self-repairs an orientation on the part of speakers to say things "just so"—to speak in a particular way. Notice that this does not mean that speakers are always endeavoring to be truthful or correct. They may just as well be designing utterances to portray themselves in a particular way, to protect themselves, to obscure information, and so on. That is, the alignments they establish, or attempt to establish, with other participants may or may not be ones of which those participants (or we) would approve.

When the recipient of an utterance initiates or completes a repair of that utterance, he or she normally does so in the second turn—the next turn after the trouble source. A typical *next turn repair initiator* (NTRI) might be a one-word question (such as "What?" "Huh?" "Who?"), a partial repeat of the trouble source with or without a question word attached ("a meeting when?" "his own paintings?"), or a question that supplies a possible clarification (Schegloff et al., 1977). C's NTRI in line 8 of the "in the dark" segment (5.11) is an example of the last. Using these and other devices, participants display that the prior turn was, in some way, problematic for them and that there is a need to improve alignment. As in the case of self-repairs, these other-initiations / repairs may indicate something other than a lack of understanding on the part of the recipient. In Data Segment 5.14, *CBS Evening News* anchor Dan Rather is interviewing (then) Vice President George Bush and focusing the talk on Bush's involvement in the Iran / Contra affair—which is what he is referring to with the expression "the record."

(5.14) [Nofsinger, 1988-1989, p. 279]
11 R: let's talk about the record.
12   You say that we've misrepresented your record
13 B: [Let's talk about the ful]l record
14 R: Let's talk about the record if we've misrepresented
15 B: [Yeh]
16 R: your record in any way (0.4) here's a chance to set it
17   straight=
18 B: =Right. I just set it straight on one count . . .

In line 13, Bush interrupts Rather with a correction of line 11 ("the record" is replaced with "the full record"). Analysis of this broadcast interview indicates that many of Bush's utterances are designed to broaden the scope of discussion beyond Iran/ Contra, thus "the *full* record" (Nofsinger, 1988-1989). So this instance of correction seems designed to change Rather's alignment toward the issues being discussed, as opposed to rectifying a mistake or misunderstanding in Rather's talk. Bush is using correction as a tactic in support of the strategy of getting *his* agenda talked about. Notice that the proposed correction is not accepted by Rather, who reverts to using "the record" in his next turn (line 14). There are several instances like this during the course of the interview, and Rather consistently avoids either saying "the full record" or talking about Bush's broader political record (Nofsinger, 1988-1989).

Schegloff et al. (1977) argue that there is a preference for self-repair in conversation (they say "self-correction"). Remember from our discussion in Chapter 3 that the technical term *preference* refers to the structure of utterances, the way turns are organized, not to participants' desires. Self-repair predominates over other-repair, according to Schegloff et al., due to the sequential positions in which repair occurs. Of the four locations in which repair routinely occurs, three of them are positions for *self*-repair: the same turn unit as the trouble source, the immediately following TRP space, and the third turn (speaker's next turn after recipient's turn). Only one of the normal repair locations is a position for the recipient of a problematic utterance to speak: the second (next) turn. Furthermore, the first two of these repair positions are for the first speaker. So the producer of the trouble source has the first two opportunities for repair and three out of the normal four. Thus the turn-taking system provides for there to be more self-repair than other-repair. One implication of this is that when this preponderance of self-repair does not occur, we are in a position to investigate what other factors (besides the turn system itself) may be operating. Zahn (1984), for example, has discovered that the type of repair (who initiates and repairs) is sensitive to the type of trouble source and the relationship history of the participants.

DELAY, REVISION, AND PREEMPTION

Sometimes, speakers sense that an action is not "going over" well and are able to change it at the last moment. This leads to a special type of repair. In Chapter 3 we saw how responses to first actions are organized by a system of preference, in which one alternative response is typically produced simply and without delay (the preferred response) and the other alternatives are typically delayed and structurally complex (dispreferred responses). When a response is delayed or otherwise marked as reluctant or dispreferred, the first speaker often projects the impending occurrence of a disagreement or other dispreferred response in time to revise his or her action. This revised action is typically designed in a way that makes it more attractive or more acceptable to the recipient. Consider Data Segment 5.15.

(5.15) [Pomerantz, 1984, p. 77]
1 B: . . . an' that's not an awful lotta fruitcake
2   (1.0)
3 B: Course it is. A little piece goes a long way.
4 A: Well that's right

Since delay is one marker of a dispreferred response, the one-second silence (line 2) allows B to project that A may be going to disagree with the assessment in line 1. B then produces a revised version of that statement before A's disagreement can occur. In this case, it preempts the impending disagreement and A responds with a preferred response, an agreement to B's revised statement. Pomerantz (1984) describes revisions such as this as "reversals" or "backdowns"; she reminds us that this is one way in which the preference system tends to result in the production of agreements over disagreements (pp. 76-77). In the terms of this chapter, a display of mutual alignment is achieved.

Participants use a similar procedure when the first speaker produces a request, invitation, offer, or similar action. In Data Segment 5.16, B offers A a coffeepot.

(5.16) [Davidson, 1984, pp. 110-111, simplified]
1 B: Do you want any pots for coffee or a ny(thing).
2 A: ⌐We:ll I have:
3   (.)
4 B: You know, I have that great big glass coffee m-
5   .hhh maker it makes ni:ne cu:ps.

Although A's talk is not delayed in this case, overlapping B's last word as it does, the second pair part (the actual response to the offer) is delayed. The "we:ll" and the short pause (line 3) are features that often accompany dispreferred second actions, and A's "I have:" could be the beginning of an account for rejecting B's offer ("I have a coffeepot"). The design of A's utterance, then, is such that B should be able to see an impending rejection of the offer. Before A actually produces that rejection, however, B revises the offer (lines 4-5), making it more specific as to the type and size of coffee maker that is being offered.

As in the case of a speaker revising an assessment or other statement, revised offers, requests, and the like are normally designed to appear more acceptable, to appear more likely to result in a preferred response, than the original offer was. The end result may be that participants are able to display themselves as mutually aligned. Notice also how much the pattern of producing a revised statement, invitation, offer, request, or the like resembles the pattern of other-initiated self-repair: We can see second-turn delay (which, in cases like the "fruitcake" example, becomes second turn omitted) as indicating trouble in the first turn. The first speaker then attempts to repair the trouble in the next available turn.

In summary, repair is initiated when a participant marks some portion of a turn as a trouble source. This is often done by the speaker of the trouble-source turn (self-initiation), but is also done by other participants (other-initiation). The repair itself can also be accomplished either by the speaker of the trouble source (self-repair) or by another (other-repair). Self-initiation/repair generally predominates in conversation because of characteristics of the turn-taking system, but the extent of this tendency remains to be documented. Repair is common in conversation. Like the other forms of alignment we have discussed, it keeps participants updated on what meanings they are conveying, what actions they are taking toward each other, and the stances from which they are operating. We need to remind ourselves, however, that repair produces *displays* of alignment rather than absolute proof that participants agree with or understand each other. For example, someone who issues a revised invitation when it appears that the initial invitation will be declined may or may not actually want the recipient to accept. What we can see in the talk is the display of a revised, more appealing invitation.

❏ Pre-Positioned Alignment Devices

Most of the alignment techniques we have examined thus far have been responses or other talk placed in a second or third turn. That is, the alignment they display is with prior utterances. While this is a routine and continuing process in conversation, participants are not limited to *retrospective* displays of alignment. They can attempt to influence the interpretation that an ongoing or future utterance will get by incorporating alignment components within that same turn, or by placing them in a prior turn. These alignment devices are designed to enhance or forestall certain reactions to the turn in which they occur, or to a later turn. Two categories of such devices, which McLaughlin (1984) reviews together under the term *preventatives*, are disclaimers and licenses (pp. 202-207).

PREVENTATIVES

In their well-known essay on *disclaimers*, Hewitt and Stokes (1975) emphasize the potential effects of talk on the social identity of the speaker and conceive of disclaimers as devices that prevent an impending action from reflecting unfavorably on its speaker. From our perspective on alignment, the function of a disclaimer is to propose what interpretation should (or should not) be given to the utterance or action that follows it. Disclaimers are expressions such as "I really don't mean to insult you, but . . . "; "Well, I'm just a computer user, not a programmer, but . . . "; and "I know it's none of my business, but . . . ." They propose that the speaker is taking a certain alignment to the talk in the rest of the turn and that recipients should take account of that alignment in their interpretation. Thus disclaimers operate *prospectively* by setting up a particular alignment to a conversational action or utterance that has not yet been produced.

In her study of *licenses*, Mura (1983) focuses on devices employed by speakers to display that an impending utterance may apparently—but only apparently—violate a common rule of conversation. She analyzes her data in terms of Grice's conversational maxims (which we discussed in Chapter 2). She describes speakers' techniques for advising other participants that, although what is about to be said may seem to violate a particular maxim, the speaker is really attempting to adhere to the cooperative principle. For example, in Data Segment 5.17, a speaker who is about to answer another's request does so in a way that warns of a problem of insufficient evidence (a potential violation of the maxim of evidence).

(5.17) [Mura, 1983, p. 108, B-K, renumbered]
1 B: Tell me what you know about weather (.) on: the
2   Pacific coast . . .
       ((two speaker turns omitted))
3 K: (I really haven't ever) studied anything that specific.
4   There are some areas, (I think more like the Los Angeles
5   area . . .)

In line 3, K prefaces her answer (a report on Pacific Coast weather) with a statement about the limits of her knowledge of the topic. Mura (1983) argues that such message components "grant a license for a violation of a maxim" (p. 104) by displaying the speaker's efforts to avoid misleading or confusing listeners—the speaker's efforts, that is, to communicate cooperatively. Note that disclaimers have been conceptualized as prefacing devices. And while this instance of licensing also precedes the talk it is designed to affect, licenses sometimes occur just at the end of the rule-violating utterance. In either case, however, they propose that the speaker's alignment to the norms of conversation is a benign one and that no serious violation is intended.

OTHER PREFACES

A variety of disclaimers and licenses has been identified, but not all alignment prefaces are designed to deal with potentially negative or discrediting outcomes. Participants often preface an utterance so as to distinguish it from prior talk, to make it more noticeable, or to display its importance. In Data Segment 5.18, an utterance that is designed to bring talk about travel plans to a close is prefaced to increase its visibility.

(5.18) [field notes]
1 N: Well listen. You folks have a good trip back.
2 M: Yeh. Thank you.

N's "Well listen" serves to draw attention to the sentence that follows. This displays the speaker's alignment to that sentence as especially noteworthy.

In Data Segment 5.19, prior utterances have alluded to the previous day as a bad day for skiing (due to poor visibility); then J relates his experience of that day.

(5.19) [Cliff Story, simplified]
56 J: Well it's amazing tha:tuh (.)
57   I picked the right day to get sick on.

58   (1.2)
59 M: Mm hmm (0.8) ((eating noises)) you sure did.

The preface (line 56) focuses increased emphasis on line 57. By using the assessment "amazing," J proposes that his statement (about getting sick on a day that was too awful for skiing anyway) deserves special emphasis and attention. That is, J displays the appropriate way for participants (including himself) to align to that statement. Goodwin and Goodwin (1987) provide a detailed discussion of ways in which same-utterance assessments create a context for the interpretation of the rest of the utterance.

PRESEQUENCES

One obvious device that displays participants' alignment to a planned future utterance is the presequence. Remember that a presequence is an adjacency pair that projects or leads up to some other action (as we discussed in Chapter 3). One kind of alignment that results from presequences is participants' alignment to each other's communicative availability. This is provided most clearly by the summons-answer sequence, as in Data Segment 5.20.

(5.20) [Nofsinger, 1973]
1 A: Hey, listen
2 B: What
3 A: Why don't we go over to . . .

B's answer (line 2) to A's summons (line 1) displays that B is available for further communication and occasions another turn by A. But the summons itself displays the availability of *its* speaker, who is expected (as a normative requirement) to speak again in the third turn (see Schegloff, 1972). Thus the mutual alignment of the participants to continuing the conversation is established.

    In Chapter 4, we drew upon Schegloff's (1980) analysis of action projections to see how a speaker could reserve an extended turn to tell a story or produce some preliminary talk that leads up to a question or other action. This, too, is a form of prospective alignment. B's action projection in Data Segment 5.21 displays the speaker's alignment to eventually producing a question.

(5.21) [Schegloff, 1980, pp. 108-109; see also Data Segment 4.5]
1 B: Now listen, Mister Crandall, let
2   me ask you this. A cab. You're
3   standing onna corner. I heardjuh
4   talking to a cab driver.
5 A: Uh::uh

The action projection ("let me ask you this") actually identifies the impending action as a question and marks the intervening talk as preliminary to that question. Notice that in this instance the action projection itself is effective—even before A's response—in aligning the participants to B's taking an extended turn. B produces and is allowed to produce three more turn construction units after the action projection before A speaks. In this case, B's action projection is as much a preface (within the same turn) as it is a presequence. In Data Segment 5.22, on the other hand, it is clearly an adjacency pair that leads up to the district attorney's action in line 3.

(5.22) [Maynard, 1984, p. 86]
1 DA: I think I've got an offer that I'll make at this time
2 PD: Sure shoot
3 DA: Um I'd offer . . .

A presequence (lines 1-2) displays the mutual alignment of the district attorney and the public defender to the impending production of an offer.

In other cases, a presequence aligns the participants to a possible future action by checking out the situation (rather than by announcing the impending action). This is illustrated in Data Segment 5.23.

(5.23) [field notes]
1 B: Uh, are you gonna have access to the car about
2   five thirty or six today
3 E: Uh:: yeah I think so. Why?
4 B: Cause I'm gonna need a ride down to . . .

Notice that the presequence (lines 1-3) displays the participants' alignment to *some* impending action involving access to
E's car, but not to a specific type of action (it could have been
an offer to wash the car rather than a request for a ride).

So speakers attempt to guide the interpretations that might
be given to their upcoming talk, to avoid negative judgments
about themselves by other participants, to emphasize the importance of a particular aspect of what they are about to say, to
ensure that their talk will be understandable (that references
will be clear and so on), or to display their own alignment
toward a particular issue. They employ disclaimers, licenses,
and other prefaces, as well as various types of presequences, to
achieve this alignment. Such prospective alignment work may
or may not reduce the need for retrospective alignment work
such as repair. More research is needed on this question.

❑ Alignment at Conversational Boundaries

Alignment work can occur anywhere in a conversation.
But it seems that special sorts of alignment would need to be
worked out just as conversations begin and as they are brought
to a close. In conversational openings, participants might have
to establish that they are mutually ready to communicate,
that they have some appropriate social relationship with each
other, what they are going to communicate about, and even
(as in the case of telephone calls) who they are. In conversational closings, participants would need to negotiate that their
conversation is coming to a close. Several strong research studies give us excellent insight into what goes on at conversational boundaries.

TELEPHONE OPENINGS

In studying a corpus of about 450 telephone calls, Schegloff
(1979, 1986) proposes that such potential problems as those
mentioned above are dealt with by four "core" opening sequences (1986, pp. 117-118). Examine Data Segment 5.24 (C is
the caller and R is the responder or answerer).

(5.24) [Schegloff, 1986, p. 115, modified]
 0 ((telephone rings))
 1 R: Hallo,
 2 C: Hello Jim?
 3 R: Yeah,
 4 C: 's Bonnie.
 5 R: Hi,
 6 C: Hi, how are yuh
 7 R: Fine, how're you,
 8 C: Oh, okay I guess
 9 R: Oh okay.
10 C: Uhm, (0.2) what are you doing New Year's Eve.

Alignment on participants' availability to talk is established, at
least initially, by a summons-answer sequence (the ringing of
the phone and R's "Hallo"). That should not surprise us, since
the summons-answer is routinely used to make contact for
purposes of conversing. Then, since neither participant can see
the other, an identification sequence aligns them to each other's
identities. Lines 2-4 could be considered the primary identification and recognition sequence, but note that R's initial "Hallo"
(line 1) provides a voice sample from which C can begin to
identify whoever answered the phone. Likewise, it is in line 5
that R displays that the caller's self-identification as "Bonnie"
is adequate for recognition purposes. So even though these core
sequences occur in an established order, their functions overlap somewhat. In face-to-face conversation the problems of
establishing availability to talk and mutual identification can
often be taken care of visually. Consequently, the exchange of
greetings tends to occur earlier than in telephone conversation

(lines 5-6 in this segment). Notice also that we do not have two sets of greetings here. The first "Hallo" is the answer to a summons and could well be accomplished with other expressions: I routinely answer the phone at the office (or even at home when I am attending to business) by saying "Bob Nofsinger." The second "Hello" (line 2) is part of the identification sequence. The participants, then, are not repeating themselves when they later say "Hi" to each other; greetings come after identification/recognition in telephone talk.

> We think of conversational openings as ritualized— this is a mistake.

After the greetings, there is an exchange of initial inquiries (often about the well-being or current activity of the conversational partner) and responses to those inquiries. In the telephone segment (5.24), this occurs in lines 6-9. Again, there is an overlap of functions at line 6, which is part greeting and part inquiry. The design of line 8, with its delay ("Oh") and its lack-of-conviction marker ("I guess"), suggests a prompt to open up C's well-being as a full-fledged topic of discussion. That is, it may be an attempt to occasion an additional inquiry about C (an "itemized news inquiry"; see Button & Casey, 1985). But R merely acknowledges C's turn—a possible indication of lack of alignment between the participants. As it turns out, the first "official" topic of the conversation, the one whose sequential location establishes it as the reason for the call, is what R has planned for New Year's Eve. We can immediately recognize line 10 as one of those prospective alignment devices, the presequence. The participants are now suitably aligned with each other for purposes of conducting a conversation (despite R's failure to pursue the issue of C's being just "Oh, okay I guess").

We tend to think of conversational openings as ritualized and perhaps even as scripted. This is a mistake for at least two reasons. First, the core sequences may be truncated (shortened) or preempted by actions that belong to the next sequence, as in Data Segment 5.25.

(5.25) [Hopper, 1989, p. 185]
1 S: Hello:?
2   (0.3)
3 J: Skeet?
4 S: Yep
5   (0.2)
6 J: Jo:hn what are you up to
7 S: How you doin

The ringing of the phone (not shown) and "Hello:?" are the summons-answer sequence, and lines 3, 4, and the first word of 6 are the identification sequence. But the exchange of greetings that would be expected at this point is missing. Furthermore, J's initial inquiry (which Hopper, 1989, says may "delete" the slot for exchange of greetings) is not followed by a typical response (such as "nothing much"), but by S's return inquiry. So in any given opening, one or more pieces of the supposed ritual may be missing. Second, the routine of opening a telephone conversation is often subtly marked to focus on a particular element or display a certain alignment (the urgency of getting to the reason for the call, the fact that the participants know each other well, or that the caller is returning an earlier call, and so on). Hopper (1989) has analyzed 25 recorded telephone openings for the ways in which they match or differ from Schegloff's (1986) model and concludes that important divergences arise for good communicative reasons. We should not hide these important details of opening design from ourselves by thinking of openings as "just ritual."

CONVERSATIONAL CLOSINGS

It is easy enough to see that special alignment procedures might be needed to begin a conversation, but why should the ending pose any problems for participants? One source of potential difficulty is that a conversation may end before participants have talked about all the matters that should be brought up in that conversation. Another is that the conditional relevance of adjacency pairs and the power of any utterance to occasion further talk may make it difficult for participants to stop. Put another way, participants have to design their talk in such a way that there is no TRP at the end of some turn, that transition to another speaker (or continuation of the same speaker) is no longer relevant. Schegloff and Sacks (1974) propose that these problems are taken care of by the participants jointly producing a closing section that consists of (at least) four turns. In the first turn, one participant produces a *preclosing* (really a possible preclosing, since the conversation might not end). This can be an utterance such as "okay," "all right," or "so:::" that does not make any substantive contribution to the topic at hand and does not solicit or initiate talk on a new topic. Other types of preclosing utterances include reiterating arrangements between the participants ("So we'll see you next week"), mentioning the reason for the conversation ("Well, I just wanted to wish you a happy birthday"), and citing some urgent requirement ("I gotta get back to work"). The speaker thereby displays that he or she has left nothing unmentioned that ought to be mentioned in that conversation (items of news, for example; Schegloff & Sacks call these "unmentioned mentionables," pp. 242-246). In this way, the speaker displays alignment to the possible closing of the conversation. In the second turn, the other participant can revert back to topical talk, with the result that either the final closing may be postponed for two or three utterances or the closing section may be halted and restarted again later (see Button, 1987). However, if the other speaker also produces a preclosing in the second turn, the participants may then move to the terminal exchange, as Data Segment 5.26 illustrates.

(5.26) [Button, 1987, p. 102]
1 G: I'll be down there, o̲h̲ en yo̲u̲'ll-
2   you'll be aroun' then when I (come in)
                                     ⌈
3 E: ⌊Yeah.
4 G: Okay.
5 E: O̲kay dear,
6 G: Buh Bye,
7 E: By̲e̲ bye,

The topic (but not necessarily the conversation) is concluded in lines 1-3. Then G and E both produce preclosings (lines 4-5), what we will call a *preclosing sequence*. Even at this point, there are techniques for moving out of the closing (Button, 1987), but none is used here. Instead, the terminal exchange (Schegloff & Sacks's term) or *terminal sequence* occurs: G and E produce the first and second parts of an adjacency pair (lines 6-7) that suspends the relevance of further talk. The ending of the conversation has been negotiated through a closing section that consists of a display of mutual alignment toward having nothing more to say (the preclosing sequence) and a mutual marking of the conversational boundary (the terminal sequence).

We should note that there are other places, besides conversational boundaries, at which special alignment requirements may arise (for example, the transition from one topic to another). There are also specialized vocal devices that may, on occasion, be used for alignment. Glenn (1989), O'Donnell-Trujillo and Adams (1983), and others have studied the coordinating and aligning functions of laughter, for example. Detailed consideration of such additional alignment practices is beyond the scope of this book.

❑ Context

Up to this point, we have made relatively little mention of the role of *context* in alignment. But to the extent that alignment processes guide participants to intersubjective understandings of each other's messages, we would assume that context plays a vital role. It turns out that we have been considering context all along. Context, in the "micro" sense of "prior conversation," is clearly and directly relevant to alignment.[4] Heritage (1984b, p. 242) says that utterances are both context-shaped and context-renewing. That is, each utterance is interpreted in the context of the talk that preceded it and forms part of the context of talk that follows it. This aspect of context is constructed, maintained, and modified turn by turn as the conversation progresses. Context, in this immediate and narrow sense, is composed not just of what people know, but of what participants *do* to show each other which items of their shared knowledge should be used in making interpretations. The conversational actions produced by participants create an interpretive resource that is used to align conversational understanding. In recent work, I have identified several practices of utterance design and sequential placement that participants use to locate and display specific items of knowledge (Nofsinger, 1989): Participants "methodically help each other to access those particular items as relevant to a specific moment of the conversation. . . . context works because it involves subtle processes of participants communicating to each other" (p. 238). It is through this conversational work, not just the fact that perceptions and knowledge are shared, that participants achieve alignment.

❑ Summary

Conversation is as smooth and effective as it is because participants continually work to make it that way, although they may not fully recognize the aligning work they are doing. In the normal course of responding to an utterance, a participant displays an understanding of that utterance for other participants to see, to evaluate, and to accept or modify. In particular, such common responses as assessments, newsmarks and "oh" receipts, continuers, and formulations have been studied and their contribution to alignment described. Any second part of an adjacency pair also displays its speaker's alignment toward the participant who produced the first pair part. The process of repair is also an important contributor to conversational alignment. Participants routinely modify or repair talk that they have just produced or talk that some other participant has just produced. Both self-repair and other-repair display an alignment toward a specific prior utterance as being "repairable" (although no actual error may noticeable in that prior talk). Self-repair predominates due to turn-taking considerations, but both types provide a mechanism for modifying the alignment between participants. Several forward-looking or prospective practices enable participants to guide the interpretation of upcoming or impending talk. The alignment roles of presequences, disclaimers, and licenses have been studied in some detail. Finally, alignment at conversational boundaries (openings and closings) is negotiated through the use of various types of adjacency pair sequences. The conduct of conversation involves ongoing efforts by the participants to update their understanding of the communication "game" in progress, both on a turn-by-turn basis and for larger segments of the conversation.

Most of our study thus far has focused on individual actions and sequences of two, three, or four actions. In Chapter 6 we will use our command of these microdetails of conversation to examine some of its larger "macro" structures, such as arguments and stories.

❏ Notes

1. That is, invitations, bets, offers, proposals, and other actions that properly take acceptances as the preferred second pair part (and rejections or declinations as dispreferred seconds) can be tentatively "identified" in the interpretation of the recipient by that person's production of an acceptance (or rejection) (see Heritage, 1984b, pp. 254-264).

2. That is, we will assume a statement rather than, say, an ironic joke that means something like "that's the last thing in the world I need." We will also assume that this utterance has not been produced in answer to a question.

3. Ragan (1983), for example, has studied this and other alignment devices in interviews.

4. Another sense of context is what we commonly think of as the institutional background of a conversation (Schegloff, 1987a). The idea is that people understand each other because of "shared" knowledge and experiences they have gained as members of the same social institution. The problem with this notion of context, as Schegloff (1987a) persuasively argues, is that it fails to address the issues of which institution (if any) is relevant to a particular conversation and how the participants know that.

6

Extended Structures

We have all encountered lengthy stories in conversation and been involved in substantial arguments with other participants. While any conversation may be quite short (one turn each by two participants, for example), and portions of conversation often comprise just one or two pairs of actions, the practical demands of everyday life often require the construction of more extended and elaborate segments of talk. When we are telling friends a detailed story of some personal experience, or negotiating a date (or other social activity), or describing our job qualifications to an interviewer, or arguing with someone who does not share our immediate concerns or point of view, we usually find ourselves taking many turns or lengthy turns, or both. In this chapter we will use the insights we have gained in preceding chapters to examine how participants put together such extended conversational structures as arguments and stories. Although we will use relatively short data segments as examples, it will be clear that the same practices

145

146 EVERYDAY CONVERSATION

employed to produce these shorter structures could be used to produce longer and more elaborate ones. To describe our task another way, we shall investigate the extended structures of conversation as turn-organized, alignment-displaying exchanges of communicative actions and sequences of actions. We begin with ordinary, everyday argument.

❏ Argument

Everyone experiences or anticipates disagreement in conversation. Sometimes disagreement is openly and clearly expressed, sometimes it occurs only indirectly, sometimes it is resolved (and sometimes not), and sometimes it is avoided. But in all these situations disagreement is *potentially* relevant to what participants do. The pioneering work on conversational argument by Jackson and Jacobs (1980) views arguments as "disagreement relevant speech events . . . characterized by the projection, avoidance, production, or resolution of disagreement" (p. 254) (see also Jacobs & Jackson, 1981). These authors treat the actions of argument in terms of speech act theory and the organization of those acts in terms of adjacency pairs, turn taking, and repair. They, and other investigators of argument, also employ a distinction between *making* an argument and *having* an argument (O'Keefe, 1977). Roughly, the first involves using reasons, evidence, claims, and the like to "make a case." The latter involves interactive disagreement (for example, "You can't," "I can," "Oh no you can't," "Well I certainly can").[1] Conversational argument often consists of participants making arguments in the process of having one. We will return to this distinction later.

Remember our discussion of *preference* in Chapter 3. The first pair part of an adjacency pair is typically designed to elicit a particular second pair part, the preferred response. Other second pair parts, although they fulfill the requirements of the adjacency pair (of conditional relevance), are dispreferred.

From the perspective of conversational organization, one way in which an argument can arise is when a first pair part fails to get a preferred second pair part in response. For example, the recipient of an invitation (which is designed to get an acceptance) either rejects that invitation or in some other way withholds the acceptance. The person issuing the invitation may then reissue it in modified form, produce reasons the other participant should accept, or attempt a repair in some other way. The basic invitation-acceptance/rejection adjacency pair is thus expanded to include more turns and perhaps more complex turns. Similarly, a request can be refused, objected to on some grounds, or treated as not justified, as in Data Segment 6.1.

(6.1) [Jacobs & Jackson, 1981, p. 124, modified]
      ((J has agreed to help L move tomorrow afternoon))
1 L: Can you be up by ten tomorrow?
2 J: Oh: man. I dunno. Why
3 L: Uh, cause Larry has to come with the van in the
4   morning rather than in the afternoon.
5 J: Oh. Tch ((pause)) hhhhh I guess so. I'll try anyway.

L's request for J to provide help starting at ten is the first part of an adjacency pair that takes an agreement as the preferred second part. That is, requests are employed to elicit agreements (and ultimately the requested behavior itself). J's response consists of elements that convey the unexpectedness of the request ("Oh man") and doubt about J's ability to comply ("I dunno"). The turn ends with a request for more information. In producing that "why" question, J treats the request as not sufficiently justified. In Chapter 2 we noted that one defining condition (constitutive rule) of a request is that the requested behavior is needed, or should be done. In conversation-analytic terms, a request to do X proposes that X needs to be done. J's line 2 calls this into question; from J's perspective, L may have produced an inappropriate request. Accordingly, the preferred second pair part is withheld and possible "disagreement," a refusal in this case, is projected. We have an argument (or one type of argument).

The dispute could be resolved in a variety of ways. L could withdraw the request ("Oh, never mind") or modify it to be more agreeable ("How about twelve-thirty?"). In this particular case, L answers J's question by producing a reason that supports the request (namely, that the van is going to be available in the morning rather than the afternoon). J then displays alignment to that reason as being sufficient and to the request as being justified by producing an agreement (line 5), although not a very wholehearted one. Notice that lines 2 and 3-4 constitute an insertion sequence within the request-agreement adjacency pair. That insertion sequence first raises and then answers an issue that needs clarification. A similar insertion sequence could directly object to the request ("That's too early") and then answer the objection (possibly in exactly the same way as lines 3-4). So an argument often involves an *expansion* of what might otherwise have been just an adjacency pair with a preferred second (Jackson & Jacobs, 1980).

Expansion need not occur from within. It can occur at the end of an adjacency pair (what Jackson & Jacobs, 1980, pp. 260-261, call a "postsequence"). This would have been the case if J had refused the request above ("Uh, no. I don't think I can make it that early") and L had then reinstituted the request by producing a reason, as in lines 3-4. This would be a request-refusal adjacency pair followed by a (possible) reinstatement-agreement pair. Expansion can also occur with presequences, as in Data Segment 6.2.

(6.2) [Jackson & Jacobs, 1980, p. 259]
     ((C is in the bathroom, S is outside))
1 S: How long are you going to be?
2 C: Quick=about two minutes.
3 S: Could you hand me that book?
4 C: No.
5 S: Why?
6 C: Just wait! I'll be done in a second.

"No I won't!"   "Oh yes you will!"
"I won't!"   "You will!"
"Won't!"   "Will!"

S's prerequest (line 1) is designed to check out the need for, and the possible success of, a request to hand a book out of the bathroom (as it turns out). Some replies to that first pair part of the presequence could have been used as support for the upcoming request (for example, "I'll be about another twenty minutes," "I need that book now, could you hand it to me?"). Such a use of the presequence to generate supporting evidence for one's next conversational action displays a concern for possible disagreement (refusal, in this case). That is, the disagreement relevance of S's talk is exhibited even before the request is actually refused in line 4. C's actual reply (line 2) to the prerequest seems designed to head off the impending request by describing the situation in a way that provides too little justification for the inconvenience. Note that such an

utterance design does not allow us to attribute such an intention to C at this point. We cannot tell from this talk alone that
C even anticipates a request. For example, line 1 could be a
preannouncement leading up to this by S: "I'm going to the
office, honey, I'll give you a kiss tonight." As it happens, S
produces a request, which C then refuses, a basic adjacency pair
(lines 3-4) that has already been "expanded" by a presequence.
But the argument is expanded even further in postsequence
position (lines 5-6). S challenges C's refusal; that is, by asking
for further clarification, S treats the refusal as not sufficiently
justified. C answers the question by employing the characterization of the situation developed in the presequence (that C
will be done very quickly). In the end, S does not withdraw the
request (even though it is not agreeable to C) and C does not
produce the preferred second pair part (the agreement sought
by S). In working through to that result, the participants expand
their talk into a more extended argument structure.

Sometimes an extended portion of conversation may not
strike us as being an argument, because of participants' friendly
tone, or because actions are designed in a questioning or "uncertainty" format. As shown in Data Segment 6.3, however, it
may still have some form of disagreement as well as other
structural similarities to more obvious arguments.

(6.3) [Cliff Story]
        ((Participants are on a ski trip; J has just joked about
        wearing dark glasses and goggles at the same time.))
   1 B: ((to J)) Don't don't I recall a time when you: uh
   2   in fact had yer dark glasses on uh under yer goggles.
   3 J: No=
   4 B: =this year (.) ₜno?
   5 J: ᶦNot that I remember.
   6 B: That never happened?
   7 J: ₜS:pecially since
   8 B: ᶦ(Tha-) that was Rob Arby.
   9 J: ₜsince I don't have any dark glasses.
  10 M: ᶦRob Arby
  11 B: That was Rob Arby.

B produces an attribution about J (that he skied wearing dark glasses under his tinted goggles), but it is prefaced with a hedge ("Don't don't I recall . . . "). This gives it the shape of a confirmation/disconfirmation question and makes it seem less assertive. J denies the attribution, completing what we might call a question-disconfirmation adjacency pair (lines 1-2 and 3). Now the thing that makes this segment worth considering as an argument is that B reinstitutes the attribution, adding one detail of the time frame, by transforming J's answer into another confirmation/disconfirmation question: "no?" J answers in the negative and we again have a question-disconfirmation adjacency pair (lines 4-5). Notice the basic technique here of expanding the disagreement by recycling it. In line 6, B raises the issue yet again, and J again begins to produce an answer (line 7), although one designed as a supporting reason rather than as a direct denial as before. The prospect of a third question-disconfirmation pair looms large. Then, overlapping J's answer, B withdraws his disagreement-provoking action. He does this by redirecting the attribution toward a nonpresent third party, "Rob Arby," a skier known to all the participants (line 8). J completes his broken-off answer using a form of repair that Schegloff (1987b) calls a recycled turn beginning (line 9), which is overlapped by M "echoing" the name. Finally, B repeats his new assertion, and the talk continues for a while about "Rob Arby's" experience with the dark glasses and goggles.

None of the participants in Data Segment 6.3 above would likely have called this stretch of talk an argument. Yet it bears striking similarities (repetition or recycling of oppositional turns, for example) to segments that participants clearly would regard as argument. One advantage to using the perspective of conversational organization is that similarities and differences among various conversational events can be examined independently of what participants (or analysts) might call them in any given case. We should also note one other point about this segment: M's entry into the "argument" serves as a reminder that multiparty (as well as two-party) disputes do occur and can be studied in the same way.

Not all arguments revolve around a failure to get the right kind of second action in response to a first (getting a "no" instead of a "yes," for example, as in the above data segments). Another way in which a conversational turn can become arguable concerns what it says, as opposed to what it does. The things to which an utterance refers, the statements it makes about them, the assumptions it takes for granted about them, and the way it describes or names them can all become the focus of argument. That is, participants sometimes disagree about the *propositional content* of a turn (see Chapter 2). In Data Segment 6.4, a man is on trial for rape and his attorney, C, is cross-examining the woman, W, who was allegedly raped.

(6.4) [Drew, 1984, pp. 12-13, simplified]
16 C: Well yuh had some uh (.) fairly lengthy conversations
17   with the defendant uh: didn' you?
        ((two lines omitted))
20   (1.0)
21 W: We:ll were all talkin'
22   (0.8)
23 C: Well you kne:w at that ti:me that the defendant was
24   in:terested (.) in you (.) didn' you?
25   (1.3)
26 W: He: asked me how I'd bin
27   (1.1)
28   j- just stuff like that

Drew (1984) analyzes in great detail how the contrasting descriptions of W's conversation with the defendant operate to portray very different versions of what happened. For our purposes, the first thing to note is that the argument occurs over disagreeing *descriptions* within each turn, rather than over dispreferred *actions* produced by those turns. C asks confirmation/disconfirmation questions (lines 16-17 and 23-24) that incorporate descriptions of the defendant's and W's behavior toward each other. In one sense, W does provide answers to those questions, but her answers "confirm" a somewhat different event. Another way of putting this would be that C and

W are *formulating* things differently. Second, notice how similar
this pattern is to the type of repair called *correction* (in this case,
a more or less embedded correction), which we discussed in
Chapter 5: W answers C's questions, but substitutes a different description of the event for the one C used. C's "some . . .
lengthy conversations with the defendant" is changed to "we
were all talkin." Third, this disagreement reappears in the next
exchange between C and W: C's description that W knew "the
defendant was interested in you" is corrected by W to "He
asked me how I'd bin." The relationship between the defense
attorney's descriptions and W's, as revealed by Drew's analysis, is that C portrays a serious (and possibly romantic) interaction between the defendant and W prior to the alleged rape,
while W's descriptions portray a casual interaction. What is
arguable to each participant in this segment is the other participant's description of that night and what such a description
implies. The argument is expanded through repeated use of
conversational correction mechanisms.

Another use to which our command of conversational organization can be put is the examination of ways in which participants might try to *avoid* arguments. One technique that has
been studied and named by Maynard (1989), the *perspective-
display sequence*, consists of one participant eliciting talk from
another concerning that other person's feelings or opinion
about something. The first participant can then either express
a similar perspective or at least avoid expressing a disagreeing
position. In Data Segment 6.5, students are discussing why they
chose to attend school in Santa Barbara.

(6.5) [Maynard, 1989, p. 97][2]
```
1  C:  Ya like it up here though?
2  A:  Yeah! I really do. It's different, I mean
3  C:  How'd ju decide to come here?
4  A:  The ar:ea.
5      (1.0)
6      [Jus-] you know, cuz it's [Sanna    Bar   ](bra)
7  C:  [(.h)]                    [Mm: that's go:od ]
8  A:  That (oughta be it). hunh=
```

9 C: =It's why I did t- we:ll, yeah, it's why I came
10   up here too.

Notice that C's initial question, the *perspective-display invitation*, suggests that an affirmative reply is expected. This question and the secondary question or *prompt* in line 3 occasion a
display of A's perspective on being "here" (lines 2, 4, and 6,
for example). Knowing A's opinion, C can then display a compatible one, as in lines 9-10. If A's response is disagreeable (that
is, A's position is one that C cannot express agreement with),
C has various options for handling that, such as asking about
something else so as to change the topic (Maynard, 1989,
pp. 103-106).

In summary, the dynamics of extended (as well as brief)
conversational argument can be understood by applying our
knowledge of ordinary conversational practices and structures
such as the turn-taking system, adjacency pair sequences, the
preference system, and repair. The degree to which a segment
of talk is an argument, the differences among various categories
of dispute, and the relative effectiveness of various conversational tactics in resolving or avoiding argument are all related
to basic conversational processes. For example, the extent to
which participants defend a potentially arguable action by
including support for it in the same turn as the action itself (as
opposed to generating support using such techniques as pre-,
insertion, and postsequences) may be related to the anticipated
characteristics of turn taking in the conversation. If a participant expects not to be able to compete freely for future turns
(because of having to defer to a more powerful participant, or
because a turn-taking system is operating that does not allow
local management of turn allocation, or whatever), he or she
may attempt to construct a viable argument in a single turn.
This suggests that the distinctions mentioned earlier in this
chapter between making and having an argument may relate
not only to the nature of the issue and the "facts" of the case, but
also to differences in the degree to which interactive processes
can be used to produce or actualize the argument. As we shall

see, even those extended conversational structures that we commonly think of as being the product of a single speaker (stories, for example) can be found upon analysis to be the joint or interactive achievements of several participants.

❏ Storytelling

Stories, as told in conversation, are produced through routine conversational processes and integrated with other conversational structures. They are part of the fabric of everyday talk. As such, they are *locally occasioned* by one or more conversational turns (Jefferson, 1978). An utterance may trigger a story for some participant, the *teller*, who will then work together with one or more other participants to set up the actual telling. This preliminary or setup work is called the story *preface* or *preface sequence* (Sacks, 1974). We will continue the practice we adopted earlier of reserving the term *sequence* for an *exchange* of speaker turns, as when the teller solicits a go-ahead from an intended recipient: "Yuh heard the news," "No, what happened?" (followed by the story). Of course, if the second speaker indicates familiarity with the event ("Yeah, I just heard"), the story may be told differently or not at all.

This illustrates one major respect in which conversational storytelling is interactive: The response of a participant in the preface sequence can have important consequences for both how and whether the story gets told. One reason for this is that stories, like other conversational messages, are *recipient designed*. A story will not be told in detail to someone who already knows it, and the telling will be modified if some of the participants either know all or part of the story or are somehow involved in the story. The status of intended recipients—how they relate to or align with the projected story—is often established in the preface sequence.

A second reason for the strong influence of recipients on storytelling is that the teller often needs an extended turn to

produce the story. We saw in Chapter 4 that the turn system for
conversation allocates one turn unit at a time (a word, a phrase)
and that the turn may switch to a different speaker at the end
of any such unit. In order to tell a coherent story longer than
one turn unit (longer, say, than one sentence) the teller needs
cooperation from the recipients in order to take an extended
turn. This cooperation can be indicated by a recipient's response in the preface sequence.

In Data Segment 6.6, two recipients occasion the storytelling
in different ways.

(6.6) [Sacks, 1974, p. 338, modified]
1 K: You wanna hear muh- eh my sister told me a story
2   last night.
3 R: I don't wanna hear it. But if you must,
4   (1.0)
5 A: What's purple an' an island. Grape (.) Britain.
6   That's what 'is sis͵ter-
7 K: ⌈No. To stun me she says uh
8   there was these three girls an' they just got married?

If we think of a story preface sequence as an adjacency pair,
we can see that the first pair part is K's offer or request to tell a
story (lines 1-2). This makes relevant some sort of acceptance
or permission (or refusal!) by the intended recipients. Here,
R "pretends" to refuse the telling of the story, but then he
"reluctantly" agrees to it (these participants are males, ages
16-17). This is the go-ahead for K to take an extended turn. It
may also display R's alignment toward K (R "giving K a bad
time," for example) or toward the attributed source of the story,
K's sister (who is 12 years old). Any teller might design a story
partly on the basis of information such as that in R's utterance.
K delays in beginning the story, and A intervenes with a joke
in the guise of a guess about the upcoming story (Sacks, 1974,
p. 344). Note that A's utterance raises again the issue we strug-
gled with in Chapter 4: What is an interruption? Judged against
normal turn-by-turn standards, A's utterance occurs in a TRP

space; but it is interruptive in the sense that it violates K's newly negotiated right to an extended turn (see Sacks, 1974). In addition to being a joke, A's utterance displays an alignment toward K or his sister (namely, that any story coming from K's sister is probably trivial). Yet A's turn also occasions the story, in the sense that K treats it as an incorrect guess deserving correction. By moving into the telling with "No. To stun me . . . ," K projects an interesting story that contrasts with A's guess (Sacks, 1974, p. 344). So the preface sequence, expanded in this case beyond its two-turn minimal size, occasions the telling proper. This story, incidentally, turns out to be a "dirty" joke designed in story form.

Preface sequences do not necessarily involve an offer or request to tell a story, but they usually include some characterization of the story. This allows recipients to judge its interest and relevance. Also, tellers sometimes preface a story without soliciting a responding turn from the intended recipient. In Data Segment 6.7, the story seems to be triggered by the preceding talk. H then prefaces the story and launches right into it in one already extended turn.

(6.7) [Jefferson, 1978, pp. 224-225]
1 F: I feel sorriest for Warren hh hh how he sits there an'
2   listens to it I don' know? But, um.
3 H: Well he must'v known what she was like before 'e
4   married 'er.
5 F: I guess. And-
6 H: <u>He</u> can be a bastard too, he uh one- one day we
7   ((story continues))

In line 6, H projects an upcoming story that will likely portray "Warren" unfavorably. She also moves right into the telling without soliciting a go-ahead from F (at least, there seems to be no audible go-ahead). Her story preface ("He can be a bastard too") does double duty. It projects the impending story and something of its character, and it stands as a claim for which the story will serve as support (shades of argument!). Perhaps this latter status reduces the need for F's "permission" for an extended turn. Even in this example, however, F cooperates with H's storytelling by not intervening after the preface: "He can be a bastard too," "I don't want to hear about it!"

One other important way in which the setting up of a story can be interactive is that there can be more than one qualified teller. For example, if the story concerns an event that two of several participants have experienced, both may be potential tellers. Another way of putting this is that even if only one actual teller emerges, he or she will be faced with two different types of recipients: a *knowing recipient*, who can be presumed to know already many of the details of the event being told, and *unknowing recipients*, who are being told the story in part because of the presumption that they do not know its details (C. Goodwin, 1987, p. 118). This raises such interactional problems as who will tell the story, how the teller will design the story for a knowing recipient as well as for unknowing ones, and how the knowing recipient (the other potential teller) will align to the story and to the teller (Mandelbaum, 1987, p. 146). Participants begin to deal with these problems in the preface sequence and continue working out their respective roles during the telling sequence itself.

Mandelbaum's (1987) research into how participants achieve their interpersonal relationships through interactive storytelling includes an analysis of how two potential tellers begin their story. In Data Segment 6.8, S is talking about going to church.

(6.8) [Mandelbaum, 1987, p. 149, modified]
```
1  S:  I have to start goin'.
2      (0.8)
3      'Cuz I'm gettin' really tense.
4      (0.4)
5  M:  Yeah
6  S:  an' that really ca::lms you
7      (0.3)
```

```
 8  N:  Yeah: it does. 'n' its like medica:₁tion
 9  S:                                ⌈I was goin'
10      cra:zy t'day. on the- on the roa::d.
11      (0.4)
12  V:  Well you know what he di:d?=
13  S:  =Wen' outa my fuckin mi:nd.=
14  V:  =He m(h)ade a right- ((story continues))
```

The story is about S turning the wrong way into a lane of on-
coming traffic. S and V were both in the car and know what
happened; M and N apparently do not know the story. The
telling is occasioned through the interactive work of S and
V. Mandelbaum (1987, pp. 149-152) describes a three-turn sequence that begins the story, consisting of a *remote approach*, a
forwarding of that approach, and a *ratifying* of the forwarding
turn. S's lines 9-10 constitute a remote approach to a story
(although Mandelbaum regards S's lines 1-3 as an even more
remote approach). That is, S has projected something "tellable,"
something out of the ordinary that some of the participants
have not heard. This not only serves to alert participants to an
impending story, it provides a partial characterization of the
story for them to examine: The story concerns S "going crazy"
on the road, and it happened "today." This characterization
allows V to recognize that she knows the story (and possibly
allows M and N to recognize that they do not know the story).
V then forwards S's remote approach with a question (line 12)
that has the potential to occasion at least two different contin-
uations or trajectories: M and N can indicate that they have
heard the story (in which case its telling will likely be modified
or forgone), or talk will progress to an actual telling. In this case,
S ratifies V's forwarding by again characterizing what happened earlier that day. Presumably, M or N could have accomplished something similar to this ratification by producing a
"No, what?" reply to V. Partly because of the sequence of three
turns, it is V who begins the detailed telling (line 14) rather
than S, who first projected it. Notice how S's remote approach
turn and V's forwarding turn together accomplish about what

A story is a joint achievement of conversational participants.

the first pair part does in a two-turn preface sequence: They project and characterize the impending story, offer to tell it, and signal the need for relaxation of the turn-taking rules. The third turn (S's line 13) then provides a go-ahead for the storytelling, just as the second part of a preface sequence often does. Mandelbaum's analysis reveals how stories can be interactively prefaced by two potential tellers as well as by a teller and potential (unknowing) recipients. The *non*tellers also participate, however, by withholding talk and perhaps by indicating their recipient status nonverbally.

So the occasioning of a story is a joint or collaborative *achievement* of conversational participants. It should not be surprising to us that the telling sequence itself is also jointly constructed. For one thing, story recipients collaborate in the telling—by withholding talk at each successive TRP, by producing overlapping appreciation tokens (such as laughter), or by producing continuers ("uh huh") or other responses that treat the teller's turn as extendible (see Sacks, 1974; Mandelbaum, 1989). Second, recipients may employ repair techniques to obtain corrections or clarifications of the telling. Third, the telling sequence may be produced by more than one teller (as Mandelbaum, 1987, demonstrates). In Data Segment 6.9, M and B ("Bob") are jointly telling a story about difficult skiing conditions due to poor visibility.

(6.9) [Cliff Story, simplified]
1 M: =What really did us in was when we were (0.6) trying
2   to find our way down (0.7) and we came upon this cliff
3   (0.7) only we didn't realize it was a cliff until Bob
4   was about two feet from the edge.
5 J: Rea:lly.
6 B: Well it's it's it's even more dramatic than that. We
7   were s:tanding at the ed⌐ge of this cliff talking
8 M: ⌊((laughter))

```
 9  B:  (.) for about forty five seconds about well should we
10  J:       ((continuing laughter))
11  B:  go down this way (.) or should we g- ((story continues))
```

Although there are several pauses in M's first turn, the one at
the beginning of line 3 stands out as a point that would probably be a TRP during normal conversational turn taking: In
addition to the pause itself, the talk just preceding it ends in a
grammatical sentence. The other participants, however, collaborate in extending M's turn by not self-selecting as next speaker.
At the end of the next turn construction unit, J does take a
speaking turn, but he uses it to produce a newsmark (line 5). In
this way, J displays that M's turn conveyed something newsworthy to him, and he occasions a continuation of the story. It
happens that the telling is taken up at this point by B, whose
turn is designed as a repair of M's turn (proposing that she
did not adequately convey the drama of the incident). Co-
tellers' turns interact to determine the trajectory of the story.
M and J further contribute to the storytelling through their
laughter; a detailed transcription of how that laughter overlaps
B's talk might reveal additional points of coordination among
their behaviors. It is even possible for an unknowing recipient
to redirect the course of a story through the use of strategi-
cally designed response turns, such as clarification questions
(Mandelbaum, 1989).

   As is the case with other conversational talk, the utterances
of a story are recipient designed. That is, they are designed to
take account of who the participants are with respect to the
story itself (for example, knowing versus unknowing recipient)
and with respect to each other (friends, strangers, relatives,
business colleagues, and so on). For example, in studying one
type of storytelling among preteen and early teenage girls from
a Black urban neighborhood, M. H. Goodwin (1982) found that
characters in the story (children from the neighborhood)—
some of whom were present during the telling—were likely to
be described in ways that were appropriate for the current conversation. That is, the descriptions used in the story seemed to

be controlled as much by the relationships among the conversational participants (and other features of the storytelling situation) as by the actual event being described. This suggests not only that social relationships influence storytelling, and probably other conversational activities as well, but that such relationships are constituted (created) in part by those activities. We shall consider this possibility shortly.

In summary, conversational stories are products of collaboration by both tellers and nontellers, knowing and unknowing participants. Tellers and recipients alike employ ordinary conversational practices of utterance design and sequencing (such as listeners withholding utterances at the TRP, or negotiating a go-ahead using a presequence); in this way they extend what otherwise might be short turns by the teller into long ones and single sequences of actions into multiple. These practices also operate when one storytelling occasions another and when stories are evaluated and ended through a resumption of turn-by-turn talk (Jefferson, 1978; Ryave, 1978; Sacks, 1974). We cannot examine these story-closing processes here.

❑ Interpersonal Relationships

Although interpersonal relationships among the participants to a conversation are not conversational structures in the same sense that arguments and stories are, they can certainly be regarded as *social* structures. Furthermore, such relationships are employed as resources during the conduct of conversation. Speakers design their utterances to invoke selected relationships among participants as being momentarily relevant to the ongoing talk; recipients infer (or remember) those relationships and use them to interpret that talk. We have already seen that certain participant identities specific to a given conversational episode can have important consequences for how conversation is conducted. For example, the roles of teller and recipient of a story, or caller and called in a telephone conversation, or interviewer and interviewee, are used and also sustained by the participants. Such participant characteristics are integral parts of conversational activities and are called *discourse identities* (C. Goodwin, 1987, p. 118). The issue we shall consider here, however, is whether the conduct of conversation might be relevant to those *social* identities involved in broader interpersonal relationships (identities such as boyfriend and girlfriend, for example).

Relationship displays may occur regardless of whether the participants intend them to.

In telling a story, expanding an argument, or producing some other conversational structure, a participant may design utterances to invoke knowledge assumed to be held in common with a specific other participant. This is some item of background knowledge or shared experience that each person "knows, presumes that the other knows, and presumes that the other presumes [that he or she knows]" (Maynard & Zimmerman, 1984, p. 303, n. 5). The other participant may then respond in a way that displays a recognition of what that knowledge is. Such an interactive display that two participants share a certain item of knowledge and thus have a "history" together may make their relationship (or some aspect of it) momentarily relevant to the conversation. For example, as the story begun in the "going crazy today on the road" segment (6.8) is continued, V and S display not only that they shared the same dangerous driving experience, but that they share a close personal relationship. V reports that "He [S] thought it was a one-way street" (Mandelbaum, 1987, pp. 162-163). Only a storyteller with some confidence about another person's private thoughts—and confidence that the other will accept the teller's version of those thoughts—would be likely to claim such intimate knowledge. Mandelbaum (1987) proposes that this "telling on behalf of another" marks V and S as a "couple" and is one way of "doing" their ongoing relationship for others to see (pp. 162-163).

Another way in which interpersonal relationships can be displayed by and made relevant for conversation is when utterances refer to or display coparticipation in activities that are assumed to be part of a particular type of relationship. In Data Segment 6.10, a female college student who has brought her "boyfriend" to visit her parents is recounting an earlier event.

(6.10) [C. Goodwin, 1987, p. 124]
1 J: We went t- I went ta bed really early.=Paul left like
2   about what.=Eleven thirty?

The repair in which the pronoun "I" is substituted for "we" allows the inference that J and "Paul" may be sleeping together, and apparently such an inference was made by her parents (C. Goodwin, 1987, p. 119). "Sleeping together" is an activity recognized to be part of a more sexually involved relationship than a mere "girlfriend-boyfriend" relationship might be. Notice also that displays of uncertainty such as J produces here can result in inferences about interpersonal relationships. By asking "Paul" what time he left and prompting him to confirm that it was about "eleven thirty," J proposes that he was there about that time. Depending upon the circumstances, such displays of copresence at a certain time of day or during certain activities might also function as displays of some type of relationship (spouses, team members, and so on). The practices by which participants refer to or formulate prior joint activities, and do so in a relatively economical manner that relies on mutually assumed knowledge, are methods for accomplishing some degree of "acquaintedness" (Maynard & Zimmerman, 1984, pp. 304-305). Conversely, participants may momentarily distance their relationship by restricting their talk to what is available in the immediate setting, what is publicly available at the moment—a display of "anonymity" (p. 305). These relationship displays may occur regardless of whether the participants intend to display themselves as having that relationship.

The study of how interpersonal relationships are publicly achieved through conversation is still in its infancy. The contributions of additional practices and structures to this process will no doubt be documented for us in the coming years. But we can see enough of what future studies might reveal to get a sense of the nonobvious ways in which conversation constitutes—actually produces—the orderliness and interpersonal relationships of everyday life that we first mentioned in Chapter 1.

❑ Final Summary

The conduct of conversation involves the operation of several systems of interactive processes, and its outcomes are profoundly dependent on those processes. Conversation is first and foremost the production by participants of social and communicative actions toward each other. The utterances that convey such actions, and the actions they are interpreted to be, are closely linked to their sequential location in the conversation. Many (though not all) conversational actions are organized into paired sequences. The system by which participants locally manage their turns at talk has important consequences for conversational order in general and action sequencing in particular. Through alignment processes, participants provide each other with ongoing indications of, and repairs to, their understanding of the talk. The more complex and extended structures of conversation (such as arguments and stories) are assembled using these basic processes. And people modify these same processes to serve in more formal, nonconversational talk. The conduct of everyday conversation forms the basis of interpersonal interaction.

❏ **Notes**

1. Schiffrin (1985) makes a related—though not identical—distinction between rhetorical and oppositional argument.

2. Talk recorded in a university laboratory; subjects were asked to "get to know one another" or to "warm up."

Appendix:
Transcribing Conventions

The primary transcription symbols used in the data segments throughout this volume are explained below. This system for transcribing talk to written form was devised by Gail Jefferson, and is more extensively explained in Atkinson and Heritage (1984, pp. ix-xvi), in Beach (1989, pp. 89-90), and elsewhere. The symbols are used to represent characteristics of talk besides the words themselves, such as silences, overlapping talk, voice intonation, and laughter. In data segments taken from published sources, transcription notation that does not follow these conventions has been modified to conform to them, where possible.

Symbol	Meaning
. . .	Ellipses indicate talk omitted from the data segment.

[ ]	Square brackets between lines or bracketing two lines of talk indicate the beginning ([) and end (]) of overlapping talk.
(0.4)	Numbers in parentheses represent silence measured to the nearest tenth of a second.
(.)	A dot enclosed in parentheses indicates a short, untimed silence (sometimes called a micropause), generally less than two- or three-tenths of a second.
end of line= =start of line	Equal signs are latching symbols. When attached to the end of one line and the beginning of another, they indicate that the later talk was "latched onto" the earlier talk with no hesitation, perhaps without even waiting the normal conversational rhythm or "beat."
<u>Wait</u> a minute	Underlining shows vocal stress or emphasis.
STOP	All-uppercase letters represent noticeable loudness.
Oh: no:::	Colons indicate an elongated syllable; the more colons, the more the syllable or sound is stretched.
Wait a mi-	A hyphen shows a sudden cutoff of speech.
This is a (rehash)	Parentheses around words indicate transcriber doubt about what those words are, as in the case of softly spoken or overlapped talk.
This is a ( )	Empty parentheses indicate that some talk was not audible or interpretable at all.
((coughing))	Double parentheses enclose transcriber comments.
When? 'ats all right. Well, I don't know,	Punctuation marks are generally used to indicate pitch level rather than sentence type. The apostrophe (') indicates missing speech sounds and normal contractions. The period indicates a drop in pitch; the question mark shows rising pitch (not necessarily a question); and the comma represents a flat pitch or a slight rising-then-falling pitch. When used, the exclamation point (!) shows "lively" or animated speech.
.hh	The h preceded by a period represents an audible inbreath. Longer sounds are transcribed using a longer string: .hhhh

hh st(h)upid	The h without a leading period represents audible exhaling, sometimes associated with laughter; and laughter itself is transcribed using "heh" or "hah" or something similar. When laugh tokens are embedded in a word, they are often represented by an h in parentheses.
pt	The letters pt by themselves represent a lip smack, which occasionally occurs just as a speaker begins to talk.
Didjuh ever hear uv 'im	Modified spelling is used to suggest something of the pronunciation.
9 A: 10 B:	For ease of identification in the discussion, speakers are identified by letters, and each line is numbered.

References

Aakhus, M. (1988). *Metacommunicative practices used to accomplish concerted social activities.* Unpublished master's thesis, Washington State University, Pullman.

Atkinson, J. M. (1982). Understanding formality: Notes on the categorization and production of "formal" interaction. *British Journal of Sociology, 33,* 86-117.

Atkinson, J. M., & Drew, P. (1979). *Order in court: The organisation of verbal interaction in judicial settings.* Atlantic Highlands, NJ: Humanities.

Atkinson, J. M., & Heritage, J. (Eds.). (1984). *Structures of social action: Studies in conversation analysis.* Cambridge: Cambridge University Press.

Austin, J. L. (1975). *How to do things with words* (2nd ed.). Cambridge, MA: Harvard University Press.

Bach, K., & Harnish, R. M. (1979). *Linguistic communication and speech acts.* Cambridge: MIT Press.

Beach, W. A. (Ed.). (1989). Sequential organization of conversational activities [Special issue]. *Western Journal of Speech Communication, 53*(2).

Beach, W. A., & Dunning, D. G. (1982). Pre-indexing and conversational organization. *Quarterly Journal of Speech, 68,* 170-185.

Bennett, A. (1981). Interruptions and the interpretation of conversation. *Discourse Processes, 4,* 171-188.

Bilmes, J. (1988). The concept of preference in conversation analysis. *Language in Society, 17,* 161-181.

Brown, P., & Levinson, S. (1978). Universals in language usage: Politeness phenomena. In E. N. Goody (Ed.), *Questions and politeness: Strategies in social interaction* (pp. 56-310). Cambridge: Cambridge University Press.

Buttny, R. (1985). Accounts as a reconstruction of an event's context. *Communication Monographs, 52,* 57-77.

Buttny, R. (1987). Sequence and practical reasoning in accounts episodes. *Communication Quarterly, 35,* 67-83.

Button, G. (1987). Moving out of closings. In G. Button & J. R. E. Lee (Eds.), *Talk and social organisation* (pp. 101-151). Clevedon, England: Multilingual Matters.

Button, G., & Casey, N. (1985). Topic nomination and topic pursuit. *Human Studies, 8,* 3-55.

Cappella, J. N., & Planalp, S. (1981). Talk and silence sequences in informal conversations III: Interspeaker influence. *Human Communication Research, 7,* 117-132.

Clayman, S. E., & Whalen, J. (1988/89). When the medium becomes the message: The case of the Rather-Bush encounter. *Research on Language and Social Interaction, 22,* 241-272.

Craig, R. T. (1986). Goals in discourse. In D. G. Ellis & W. A. Donohue (Eds.), *Contemporary issues in language and discourse processes* (pp. 257-273). Hillsdale, NJ: Lawrence Erlbaum.

Craig, R. T., & Tracy, K. (Eds.). (1983a). *Conversational coherence: Form, structure, and strategy.* Beverly Hills, CA: Sage.

Craig, R. T., & Tracy, K. (1983b). Introduction. In R. T. Craig & K. Tracy (Eds.), *Conversational coherence: Form, structure, and strategy* (pp. 10-22). Beverly Hills, CA: Sage.

Davidson, J. (1984). Subsequent versions of invitations, offers, requests, and proposals dealing with potential or actual rejection. In J. M. Atkinson & J. Heritage (Eds.), *Structures of social action: Studies in conversation analysis* (pp. 102-128). Cambridge: Cambridge University Press.

Dindia, K. (1987). The effects of sex of subject and sex of partner on interruptions. *Human Communication Research, 13,* 345-371.

Douglas, J. D. (1970). *Understanding everyday life.* Chicago: Aldine.

Drew, P. (1984, August). *Disputes in courtroom cross-examination: "Contrasting versions."* Unpublished manuscript, University of York.

Drummond, K. (1989). A backward glance at interruptions. *Western Journal of Speech Communication, 53,* 150-166.

Duncan, S., Jr. (1972). Some signals and rules for taking speaking turns in conversations. *Journal of Personality and Social Psychology, 23,* 283-292.

Duncan, S., Jr. (1973). Toward a grammar for dyadic conversation. *Semiotica, 9,* 29-46.

Duncan, S. Jr., & Fiske, D. W. (1977). *Face-to-face interaction: Research, methods, and theory.* Hillsdale, NJ: Lawrence Erlbaum.

Frankel, R. M. (1989). "I wz wondering—uhm could Raid uhm effect the brain permanently d'y know?" Some observations on the intersection of speaking and writing in calls to a poison control center. *Western Journal of Speech Communication, 53,* 195-226.

Geis, M. L. (1982). *The language of television advertising.* New York: Academic Press.

Glenn, P. J. (1989). Initiating shared laughter in multi-party conversations. *Western Journal of Speech Communication, 53,* 127-149.

Goffman, E. (1971). *Relations in public.* New York: Harper & Row.

Goffman, E. (1981). *Forms of talk.* Philadelphia: University of Pennsylvania Press.

Goldberg, J. (1975). A system for the transfer of instructions in natural settings. *Semiotica, 14,* 269-296.

Goodwin, C. (1986). Between and within: Alternative sequential treatments of continuers and assessments. *Human Studies, 9,* 205-217.

Goodwin, C. (1987). Forgetfulness as an interactive resource. *Social Psychology Quarterly, 50,* 115-130.

Goodwin, C., & Goodwin, M. H. (1987). Concurrent operations on talk: Notes on the interactive organization of assessments. *IPRA Papers in Pragmatics, 1,* 1-54.

Goodwin, M. H. (1982). "Instigating": Storytelling as social process. *American Ethnologist, 9,* 799-819.

Greatbatch, D. (1986). Aspects of topical organization in news interviews: The use of agenda shifting procedures by interviewees. *Media, Culture, and Society, 8,* 441-455.

Greatbatch, D. (1988). A turn-taking system for British news interviews. *Language in Society, 17,* 401-430.

Grice, H. P. (1975). Logic and conversation. In P. Cole & J. L. Morgan (Eds.), *Syntax and semantics: Vol. 3. Speech acts* (pp. 41-58). New York: Academic Press.

Grice, H. P. (1978). Further notes on logic and conversation. In P. Cole (Ed.), *Syntax and semantics: Vol. 9. Pragmatics* (pp. 113-128). New York: Academic Press.

Heritage, J. (1984a). A change-of-state token and aspects of its sequential placement. In J. M. Atkinson & J. Heritage (Eds.), *Structures of social action: Studies in conversation analysis* (pp. 299-345). Cambridge: Cambridge University Press.

Heritage, J. (1984b). *Garfinkel and ethnomethodology.* Cambridge: Polity.

Heritage, J. (1985). Analyzing news interviews: Aspects of the production of talk for an overhearing audience. In T. A. van Dijk (Ed.), *Handbook of discourse analysis: Vol. 3. Discourse and dialogue* (pp. 95-117). London: Academic Press.

Heritage, J. (1988). Explanations as accounts: A conversation analytic perspective. In C. Antaki (Ed.), *Analysing everyday explanation* (pp. 127-144). London: Sage.

Heritage, J., & Watson, D. R. (1979). Formulations as conversational objects. In G. Psathas (Ed.), *Everyday language: Studies in ethnomethodology* (pp. 123-162). New York: Irvington.

Heritage, J., & Watson, D. R. (1980). Aspects of the properties of formulations in natural conversations: Some instances analyzed. *Semiotica, 30,* 245-262.

Hewitt, J. P., & Stokes, R. (1975). Disclaimers. *American Sociological Review, 40,* 1-11.

Hopper, R. (1989). Speech in telephone openings: Emergent interaction v. routines. *Western Journal of Speech Communication, 53,* 178-194.

Jackson, S., & Jacobs, S. (1980). Structure of conversational argument: Pragmatic bases for the enthymeme. *Quarterly Journal of Speech, 66*, 251-265.

Jacobs, S. (1985). Language. In M. L. Knapp & G. R. Miller (Eds.), *Handbook of interpersonal communication* (pp. 313-343). Beverly Hills, CA: Sage.

Jacobs, S., & Jackson, S. (1981). Argument as a natural category: The routine grounds for arguing in conversation. *Western Journal of Speech Communication, 45*, 118-132.

Jacobs, S., & Jackson, S. (1983a). Speech act structure in conversation: Rational aspects of pragmatic coherence. In R. T. Craig & K. Tracy (Eds.), *Conversational coherence: Form, structure, and strategy* (pp. 47-66). Beverly Hills, CA: Sage.

Jacobs, S., & Jackson, S. (1983b). Strategy and structure in conversational influence attempts. *Communication Monographs, 50*, 285-304.

Jefferson, G. (1978). Sequential aspects of story telling in conversation. In J. Schenkein (Ed.), *Studies in the organization of conversational interaction* (pp. 219-248). New York: Academic Press.

Jefferson, G. (1986). Notes on "latency" in overlap onset. *Human Studies, 9*, 153-183.

Jefferson, G. (1987). On exposed and embedded correction in conversation. In G. Button & J. R. E. Lee (Eds.), *Talk and social organisation* (pp. 86-100). Clevedon, England: Multilingual Matters.

Jefferson, G., & Schenkein, J. (1978). Some sequential negotiations in conversation: Unexpanded and expanded versions of projected action sequences. In J. Schenkein (Ed.), *Studies in the organization of conversational interaction* (pp. 155-172). New York: Academic Press.

Karp, D. A., & Yoels, W. C. (1986). *Sociology and everyday life.* Itasca, IL: Peacock.

Kennedy, C. W., & Camden, C. T. (1983). A new look at interruptions. *Western Journal of Speech Communication, 47*, 45-58.

Leiter, K. (1980). *A primer on ethnomethodology.* New York: Oxford University Press.

Lerner, G. H. (1987, August 27-30). *On the syntax of sentences-in-progress.* Paper presented at the Eighth International Conference for Ethnomethodology and Conversation Analysis, Boston University.

Lerner, G. H. (1989). Notes on overlap management in conversation: The case of delayed completion. *Western Journal of Speech Communication, 53*, 167-177.

Levinson, S. C. (1983). *Pragmatics.* Cambridge: Cambridge University Press.

Mandelbaum, J. (1987). Couples sharing stories. *Communication Quarterly, 35*, 144-170.

Mandelbaum, J. (1989). Interpersonal activities in conversational storytelling. *Western Journal of Speech Communication, 53*, 114-126.

Maynard, D. W. (1984). *Inside plea bargaining: The language of negotiation.* New York: Plenum.

Maynard, D. W. (1989). Perspective-display sequences in conversation. *Western Journal of Speech Communication, 53*, 91-113.

Maynard, D. W., & Zimmerman, D. H. (1984). Topical talk, ritual and the social organization of relationships. *Social Psychology Quarterly, 47*, 301-316.

McLaughlin, M. L. (1984). *Conversation: How talk is organized.* Beverly Hills, CA: Sage.

McLaughlin, M. L., & Cody, M. J. (1982). Awkward silences: Behavioral anteced-
ents and consequences of the conversational lapse. *Human Communication Research, 8,* 299-316.

Morris, G. H. (1985). The remedial episode as a negotiation of rules. In R. L. Street, Jr., & J. N. Cappella (Eds.), *Sequence and pattern in communicative behaviour* (pp. 70-84). London: Edward Arnold.

Morris, G. H., & Hopper, R. (1980). Remediation and legislation in everyday talk: How communicators achieve consensus. *Quarterly Journal of Speech, 66,* 266-274.

Motley, M. T. (1990). On whether one can(not) not communicate: An examina-tion via traditional communication postulates. *Western Journal of Speech Com-munication, 54,* 1-20.

Mura, S. S. (1983). Licensing violations: Legitimate violations of Grice's conver-sational principle. In R. T. Craig & K. Tracy (Eds.), *Conversational coherence: Form, structure, and strategy* (pp. 101-115). Beverly Hills, CA: Sage.

Nofsinger, R. E. (1973). *The demand ticket: Getting the floor to speak.* Unpublished doctoral dissertation, University of Iowa, Iowa City.

Nofsinger, R. E. (1976). On answering questions indirectly: Some rules in the grammar of doing conversation. *Human Communication Research, 2,* 172-181.

Nofsinger, R. E. (1988-1989). "Let's talk about the record": Contending over topic redirection in the Rather/Bush interview. *Research on Language and Social Interaction, 22,* 273-291.

Nofsinger, R. E. (1989). Collaborating on context: Invoking alluded-to shared knowledge. *Western Journal of Speech Communication, 53,* 227-241.

O'Donnell-Trujillo, N., & Adams, K. (1983). Heheh in conversation: Some coor-dinating accomplishments of laughter. *Western Journal of Speech Communica-tion, 47,* 175-191.

O'Keefe, D. J. (1977). Two concepts of argument. *Journal of the American Forensic Association, 13,* 121-128.

Pomerantz, A. (1978). Compliment responses: Notes on the co-operation of multiple constraints. In J. Schenkein (Ed.), *Studies in the organization of con-versational interaction* (pp. 79-112). New York: Academic Press.

Pomerantz, A. (1984). Agreeing and disagreeing with assessments: Some fea-tures of preferred/dispreferred turn shapes. In J. M. Atkinson & J. Heritage (Eds.), *Structures of social action: Studies in conversation analysis* (pp. 57-101). Cambridge: Cambridge University Press.

Pomerantz, A. (1989). Epilogue. *Western Journal of Speech Communication, 53,* 242-246.

Psathas, G. (1986). Some sequential structures in direction-giving. *Human Stud-ies, 9,* 231-246.

Ragan, S. L. (1983). Alignment and conversational coherence. In R. T. Craig & K. Tracy (Eds.), *Conversational coherence: Form, structure, and strategy* (pp. 157-171). Beverly Hills, CA: Sage.

The Rather/Bush "Interview." (1988-1989). *Research on Language and Social In-teraction, 22,* 318-326.

Roger, D. B., & Schumacher, A. (1983). Effects of individual differences on dyadic conversational strategies. *Journal of Personality and Social Psychology, 45,* 700-705.

Rosenfield, L. W., Hayes, L. S., & Frentz, T. S. (1976). *The communicative experience.* Boston: Allyn & Bacon.

Ryave, A. L. (1978). On the achievement of a series of stories. In J. Schenkein (Ed.), *Studies in the organization of conversational interaction* (pp. 113-132). New York: Academic Press.

Sacks, H. (1974). An analysis of the course of a joke's telling in conversation. In R. Bauman & J. Sherzer (Eds.), *Explorations in the ethnography of speaking* (pp. 337-353). Cambridge: Cambridge University Press.

Sacks, H. (1987). On the preferences for agreement and contiguity in sequences in conversation [from a tape recording of a public lecture originally delivered in 1973]. In G. Button & J. R. E. Lee (Eds.), *Talk and social organisation* (pp. 54-69). Clevedon, England: Multilingual Matters.

Sacks, H., & Schegloff, E. A. (1979). Two preferences in the organization of reference to persons in conversation and their interaction. In G. Psathas (Ed.), *Everyday language: Studies in ethnomethodology* (pp. 15-21). New York: Irvington.

Sacks, H., Schegloff, E. A., & Jefferson, G. (1974). A simplest systematics for the organization of turn-taking for conversation. *Language, 50,* 696-735.

Sacks, H., Schegloff, E. A., & Jefferson, G. (1978). A simplest systematics for the organization of turn-taking for conversation. In J. Schenkein (Ed.), *Studies in the organization of conversational interaction* (pp. 7-55). New York: Academic Press.

Schegloff, E. A. (1972). Sequencing in conversational openings. In J. J. Gumperz & D. Hymes (Eds.), *Directions in sociolinguistics* (pp. 346-380). New York: Holt, Rinehart & Winston.

Schegloff, E. A. (1979). Identification and recognition in telephone conversation openings. In G. Psathas (Ed.), *Everyday language: Studies in ethnomethodology* (pp. 23-78). New York: Irvington.

Schegloff, E. A. (1980). Preliminaries to preliminaries: "Can I ask you a question?" *Sociological Inquiry, 50,* 104-152.

Schegloff, E. A. (1982). Discourse as an interactional achievement: Some uses of "uh huh" and other things that come between sentences. In D. Tannen (Ed.), *Analyzing discourse: Text and talk* (Georgetown University Roundtable on Languages and Linguistics, 1981) (pp. 71-93). Washington, DC: Georgetown University Press.

Schegloff, E. A. (1986). The routine as achievement. *Human Studies, 9,* 111-151.

Schegloff, E. A. (1987a). Between micro and macro: Contexts and other connections. In J. C. Alexander, B. Giesen, R. Munch, & N. J. Smelser (Eds.), *The micro-macro link* (pp. 207-234). Berkeley: University of California Press.

Schegloff, E. A. (1987b). Recycled turn beginnings: A precise repair mechanism in conversation's turn-taking organisation. In G. Button & J. R. E. Lee (Eds.), *Talk and social organisation* (pp. 70-85). Clevedon, England: Multilingual Matters.

Schegloff, E. A. (1988). On an actual virtual servo-mechanism for guessing bad news: A single case conjecture. *Social Problems, 35,* 442-457.

Schegloff, E. A. (1988-1989). From interview to confrontation: Observations of the Bush/Rather encounter. *Research on Language and Social Interaction, 22,* 215-240.

Schegloff, E. A., Jefferson, G., & Sacks, H. (1977). The preference for self-correction in the organization of repair in conversation. *Language, 53*, 361-382.

Schegloff, E., & Sacks, H. (1973). Opening up closings. *Semiotica, 7*, 289-327.

Schegloff, E., & Sacks, H. (1974). Opening up closings. In R. Turner (Ed.), *Ethnomethodology: Selected readings* (pp. 233-264). Baltimore: Penguin.

Schiffrin, D. (1985). Everyday argument: The organization of diversity in talk. In T. A. van Dijk (Ed.), *Handbook of discourse analysis: Vol. 3. Discourse and dialogue* (pp. 35-46). London: Academic Press.

Scott, M., & Lyman, S. (1968). Accounts. *American Sociological Review, 33*, 46-62.

Searle, J. R. (1969). *Speech acts.* Cambridge: Cambridge University Press.

Searle, J. R. (1979). *Expression and meaning.* Cambridge: Cambridge University Press.

Shimanoff, S. (1980). *Communication rules: Theory and research.* Beverly Hills, CA: Sage.

Stokes, R., & Hewitt, J. P. (1976). Aligning actions. *American Sociological Review, 41*, 838-849.

Stubbs, M. (1983). *Discourse analysis.* Chicago: University of Chicago Press.

Tannen, D. (1984). *Conversational style: Analyzing talk among friends.* Norwood, NJ: Ablex.

Tannen, D. (1986). *That's not what I meant!* New York: William Morrow.

West, C., & Zimmerman, D. H. (1983). Small insults: A study of interruptions in cross-sex conversations between unacquainted persons. In B. Thorne, C. Kramarae, & N. Henley (Eds.), *Language, gender, and society* (pp. 102-117). Rowley, MA: Newbury House.

Whalen, J., Zimmerman, D. H., & Whalen, M. R. (1988). When words fail: A single case analysis. *Social Problems, 35*, 335-362.

Whalen, M. R., & Zimmerman, D. H. (1987). Sequential and institutional contexts in calls for help. *Social Psychology Quarterly, 50*, 172-185.

Wiemann, J. M. (1977). Explication and test of a model of communicative competence. *Human Communication Research, 3*, 195-213.

Wiemann, J. M. (1985). Interpersonal control and regulation in conversation. In R. L. Street, Jr., & J. N. Cappella (Eds.), *Sequence and pattern in communicative behaviour* (pp. 85-102). London: Edward Arnold.

Wilson, T. P., Wiemann, J. M., & Zimmerman, D. H. (1984). Models of turn taking in conversational interaction. *Journal of Language and Social Psychology, 3*, 159-183.

Wittgenstein, L. (1958). *Philosophical investigations* (2nd ed.). Oxford: Basil Blackwell.

Zahn, C. J. (1984). A reexamination of conversational repair. *Communication Monographs, 51*, 56-66.

Index

About the Author

Robert E. Nofsinger (Ph.D., University of Iowa) is Associate Professor in the School of Communication, Washington State University. He teaches language behavior, conversation analysis, and interpersonal and small group communication. His research interests focus on the strategic and tactical organization of conversation and other types of interactive talk, such as broadcast news interviews and talk shows, and courtroom communication. Recent published examples of this research include a study of participants' construction of conversational context through invoking shared knowledge, and an analysis of the 1988 news interview between Dan Rather and (then) Vice President George Bush. Dr. Nofsinger has served on the editorial boards of *Communication Monographs*, *Communication Reports*, and the *Western Journal of Speech Communication*. He is a member of the Speech Communication Association, the Western States Communication Association, and the Northwest Communication Association (of which he is a past president). He joined the faculty at Washington State in 1976.